Authentic Fr...
for GC...

John Creighton

Basil Blackwell

Reprinted 1991

Published by Basil Blackwell Ltd
108 Cowley Road
Oxford OX4 1JF
England

British Library Cataloguing in Publication Data
Creighton, John
Reading authentic French for GCSE.
1. French language—Examinations, questions, etc.
I. Title
448.2'421 PC2112

ISBN 0–631–90147–7

Designed by Bob Prescott
Typeset by Photo-Graphics in Bembo and Univers
Printed in Hong Kong by Wing King Tong Co. Ltd.

Acknowledgements

Unless otherwise indicated, all photographs in this book were taken by the author and remain the copyright of John Creighton.

We would like to thank the following for material reproduced in the book

Air France (24); BBC Hulton Picture Library (69F); British Caledonian Airways (25); Brittany Ferries (29, 120): Jive Records (69E); KD German Rhine Line (79); *La Semaine dans le Boulonnais* (111); *Le Monde* (59, 60, 65, 111, 112, 113, 117, 118, 119); *L'officiel des spectacles* (63, 64); *Le Republicain Lorrain* (115); *Marie-France* (58, 126); Metro/RER (21, 22, 23); *Nice-Matin* (61, 62, 66, 116, 117); North Sea Ferries (27); RATP (14, 16, 17); Rex Features Ltd (121); SNCF/CAV (19, 20).

Introduction

This book presents a collection of authentic French materials (including photographs, press cuttings, timetables, signs, newspaper and magazine articles. . .) and shows situations and language found throughout France. The materials will enable you to develop a realistic impression of life in contemporary France and, at the same time, to practise the sort of questions you will meet in the GCSE examination. The materials and exercises will also help you communicate more effectively in French if you visit France or write to a French person.

There are three main sections in this book:

Section 1 relates to everyday life—travel, shopping, entertainment, eating, going on holiday. . . The materials range from road signs to timetables, from tickets to menus.

Section 2 has a wide range of letters and postcards. Some are informal letters, written between friends. Others are more formal, making hotel bookings or business arrangements.

Section 3 contains extracts from French newspapers, magazines and other printed sources, including weather reports and technical writing.

Within each section the material is graded according to difficulty (starting with easier pieces) so you can determine your own rate of progress. Remember that in order to understand the material you do not need to know the meaning of *every* word. Use the context to help you and consider the questions after each item in logical order, as this will help you build up your understanding.

Most of the questions ask you to answer in English, but a few ask you to give the answer in French. You can answer either orally or in written form (unless specifically told to do one or the other). Your answers don't have to be complete sentences, but make sure that you have included all the relevant information.

Contents

Motoring

Road signs

1 You have just arrived in France and see signs **A** and **B**. Where would you arrive if you followed the directions of each of the signs?

A

B

2 Your Dad is driving through a French town and sees sign **C**. What does it mean?

C

3 In addition to the Car Ferry, what other two places are indicated by the signpost in **D**?

D

4 What does road sign **E** tell bus drivers?

5 You are driving in France and see sign **F**. Does it mean:
- **a** Carry on
- **b** Look out for trains
- **c** You have right of way
- **d** Give way to traffic from the right?

6 Drivers in France often come across sign **G**. It tells them:
- **a** To give way to all traffic
- **b** To slow down
- **c** Not to overtake
- **d** They have right of way at crossroads?

7 When approaching sign **H** a French driver would have to:
- **a** Stop
- **b** Allow pedestrians to cross
- **c** Give way at the junction
- **d** Slow down?

8 Which of these phrases best describes what is ahead if you see sign **I**:
- **a** Voie pour autobus
- **b** Interdit aux véhicules
- **c** Un quai
- **d** L'approche des intersections?

E

F

G

H

I

Parking

1 **A** is a common sign in France. If you were advising a lorry driver, would you say that heavy goods vehicles could park here? Give a reason.
2 Your Dad wants to park on the left-hand side of the street where there is plenty of room. According to sign **B** is he allowed to do this?
3 What do the two signs in **C** tell drivers?

A

B

C

4 What is forbidden by **D** and why?

5 What is the owner of the premises in **E** requesting, and what reason does he give?

D

E

F

PIETONS

**Pour traverser –
appuyez sur ce bouton.
Attendez l'arrêt des
voitures.**

G

**INTERDICTION ABSOLUE
DE
TRAVERSER
SANS UTILISER LES SIGNAUX**

6 Where would you find a notice like **F**? What two instructions are given?

7 What is forbidden by **G**?

8 Driving around a French town looking for a parking space you see signs **H** and **I**. What exactly does each one mean?

H

I

9 If your Dad saw sign **J** while driving in France, why would he find it a welcome sight?

J

At the garage

1 Look at **A**. Would you say this petrol pump sells 2-star or 4-star?

2 You are on holiday in France with your parents and stop at a service station, next to petrol pump **B**.

- **a** What type of fuel is on sale here?
- **b** Explain the three lines of instructions on either side of the figures.

3 At the same service station you notice pump **C**:

- **a** What grades of petrol are on sale here?
- **b** What is the smallest quantity you could buy?

4 Your family car pulls up at a self-service petrol pump. The instructions for use are jumbled up. Try to put them in the correct order:

- **a** Le placer dans le réservoir.
- **b** Présentez-vous à la caisse.
- **c** Décrochez le robinet.
- **d** Ouvrir le robinet—le maintenir ouvert jusqu'à distribution complète.
- **e** Dès que les compteurs volume et prix sont à zéro—servez-vous.
- **f** Raccrochez dès que la distribution est terminée.

5 **D** is a coin-operated self-service pump:

- **a** What does the writing to the left of the display area mean?
- **b** How much would 10 litres cost?
- **c** What do you understand by 'mélange 4% d'huile'?

6 Stopping at a garage you notice sign **E**. Can you match up the French words with these? tyres, car wash, oil, workshops, shock absorbers.

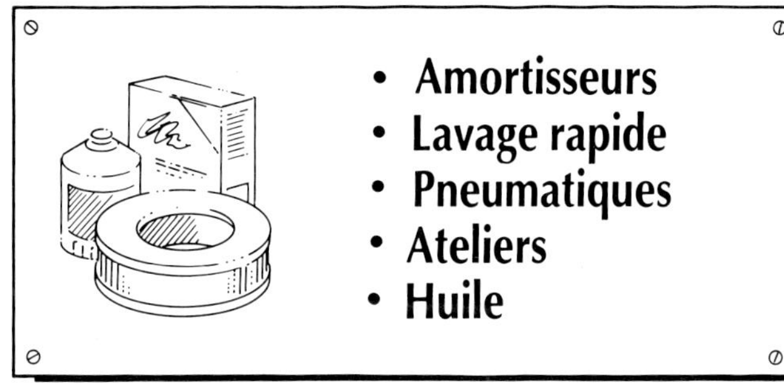

E

Other signs

1 Read extract **A** from a sign designed to help motorway drivers. What specific information is required in 2 and 3?

A

POUR FORMULER VOTRE APPEL, SIGNALEZ DANS L'ORDRE:

1 Votre identité
2 Votre position
*** sens de circulation**
*** no de borne d'appel d'urgence**
*** distance de votre véhicule par rapport à la borne d'appel d'urgence**
3 Le type de votre véhicule:
*** sa marque**
*** son immatriculation**
*** sa couleur**
4 Le type de panne, si vous avez pu l'identifier

2 The instructions in **B** are found at automatic motorway toll stations. Read them through, then put them into English.

B

Péage automatique (jet de pièces)

6, 5 — Préparez votre monnaie

Péage au guichet

40 — Gare de péage d'entrée: vous prenez un ticket.
Gare de sortie: vous rendez votre ticket et réglez le montant indiqué sur le tableau lumineux

Calculez votre tarif

Exemple:
Mulhouse-Lyon. 9 + 88 = 97FF

3 Look carefully at sign **C**:

a On what sort of building would you expect to find it?

b What happens at 8 o'clock, 9.30 and 11 o'clock?

c What would you find by turning left and travelling 400 metres?

4 Notice **D** is found outside French toilets:
  a What must you do first?
  b What happens after you leave the toilet?

5 Lamppost **E** carries several signs. Look at them carefully and answer these questions.
  a Which towns would you reach by turning right?
  b Which direction would you take to go to: the Town Hall? the Sub-Préfecture?
  c If you followed the directions on the bottom sign, which three places could you go to?
  d If you went shopping at Wierre's what would you expect to buy?
  e Which of these phrases matches the time shown by the clock:
  il est onze heures
  il est neuf heures et quart
  il est huit heures vingt
  il est onze heures vingt-cinq?

D

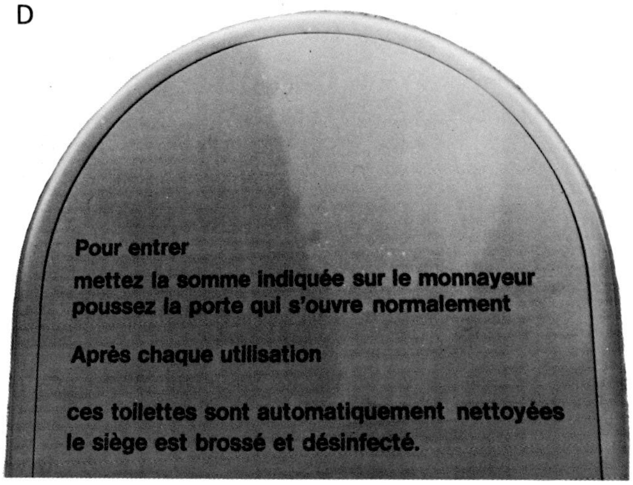

E

Bus travel

Tickets

1 While on holiday in France your friend tries to board a bus using the doors in **A**. Why would you stop her?
2 If you wished to buy a ticket, would you board to the left or right of door **B**?

A

B

3 Would bus **C** be of any use if you wished to go to the railway station?

C

4 What is the difference between bus stops **D** and **E**?
5 When would buses not stop at **F**?

D

E

F

6 Look at advertisement **G** for 'Formule 1'. What does it tell you?

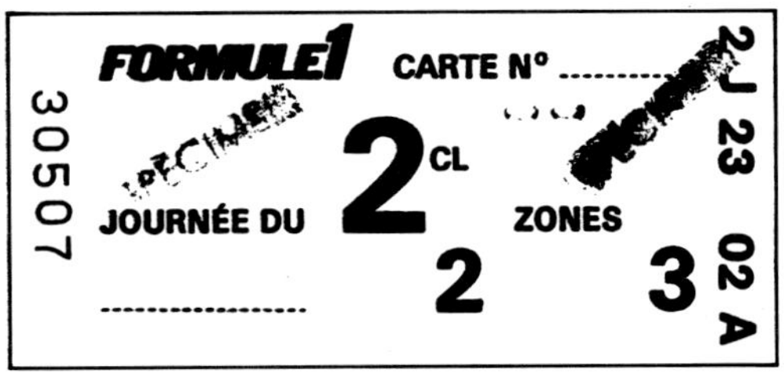

G

7 When you return to England after a holiday in Paris you show some friends tickets **H**, **J**, **K** and **L**:

- **a** On which three forms of transport could you travel with ticket **H**?
- **b** Where must you not use ticket **J**?
- **c** Explain the difference between ticket **K** and ticket **H**.
- **d** How do you know that **L** is a half-price ticket?

H

J

K

L

Timetables

While staying for a week's holiday in Boulogne you decide to visit neighbouring towns. You look at timetable **A**.

1 How long would a weekday journey from Boulogne to Wimereux Baston take?

2 If you had to meet a friend at Wimereux Centre at 1.00 pm on Tuesday, which would be the most suitable bus from Boulogne?

3 Your friend in Wimille wishes to see a film in Boulogne that starts at 21.00 and finishes at 23.00. Could he catch a bus from Wimille and one back home on a weekday?

4 On which days is there a bus at 2 o'clock from Wimereux Bon Air?

5 What do you notice about journey times during the week compared with those on Sundays?

6 What would the driver's attitude be to running late?

7 You are waiting at a bus stop when a French person asks you these questions. Reply in French.

- **a** Combien de temps met le bus pour aller de Wimereux Centre à Boulogne?
- **b** Le premier car de Boulogne à Wimereux Centre part à quelle heure?
- **c** A quelle heure part le dernier bus de Wimereux à Boulogne le dimanche?

A

HORAIRES AUX PRINCIPAUX ARRÊTS

SEMAINE

ALLER

Wimereux Baston	Wimereux Centre	Wimille Centre	Bon Secours	Boulogne Centre
6.00	6.05	6.10	6.20	6.35
6.25	6.30	6.35	6.45	7.00
6.55	7.00	7.05	7.15	7.30
7.15	7.20	7.25	7.35	7.50
8.00	8.05	8.10	8.20	8.35
8.45	8.50	8.55	9.05	9.20
9.30	9.35	9.40	9.50	10.05
10.15	10.20	10.25	10.35	10.50
11.00	11.05	11.10	11.20	11.35
12.00	12.05	12.10	12.20	12.35
13.05	13.10	13.15	13.25	13.40
14.15	14.20	14.25	14.35	14.50
15.00	15.05	15.10	15.20	15.35
15.45	15.50	15.55	16.05	16.20
16.30	16.35	16.40	16.50	17.05
17.15	17.20	17.25	17.35	17.50
18.15	18.20	18.25	18.35	18.50
19.00	19.05	19.10	19.20	19.35
20.00	20.05	20.10	20.20	20.35

RETOUR

Boulogne Pl. France	Bon Secours	Wimille Centre	Wimereux Centre	Wimereux Baston
6.25	6.35	6.45	6.50	6.55
7.15	7.25	7.35	7.40	7.45
8.00	8.10	8.20	8.25	8.30
8.40	8.50	9.00	9.05	9.10
9.30	9.40	9.50	9.55	10.00
10.15	10.25	10.35	10.40	10.45
11.00	11.10	11.20	11.25	11.30
12.10	12.20	12.30	12.35	12.40
13.30	13.40	13.50	13.55	14.00
14.15	14.25	14.35	14.40	14.45
15.00	15.10	15.20	15.25	15.30
15.45	15.55	16.05	16.10	16.15
16.30	16.40	16.50	16.55	17.00
17.20	17.30	17.40	17.45	17.50
18.15	18.25	18.35	18.40	18.45
19.15	19.25	19.35	19.40	19.45

DIMANCHE ET FETES

ALLER

Wimereux Bon Air	Wimille Centre	Bon Secours	Boulogne Centre ville
11.00	11.05	11.15	11.30
12.00	12.05	12.15	12.30
13.00	13.05	13.15	13.30
14.00	14.05	14.15	14.30
15.00	15.05	15.15	15.30
16.00	16.05	16.15	16.30
17.00	17.05	17.15	17.30
18.00	18.05	18.15	18.30
19.00	19.05	19.15	19.30
19.55	20.00	20.10	20.25

RETOUR

Boulogne Pl. France	Bon Secours	Wimille Centre	Wimereux Bon Air
10.30	10.40	10.50	10.55
11.30	11.40	11.50	11.55
12.30	12.40	12.50	12.55
13.30	13.40	13.50	13.55
14.30	14.40	14.50	14.55
15.30	15.40	15.50	15.55
16.30	16.40	16.50	16.55
17.30	17.40	17.50	17.55
18.30	18.40	18.50	18.55
19.25	19.35	19.45	19.50

Cet horaire vous est donné à titre indicatif. Des problèmes de circulation peuvent provoquer de légers retards que le conducteur est le premier à déplorer.
Ne lui en veuillez pas de quelques minutes d'attente car il fait le maximum pour vous satisfaire.

A

L'autobus standard

Moteur diesel 6 cylindres. Puissance nominale: 160 ch à 2500 tr/min; puissance d'utilisation: 144 ch à 2500 tr/min.

- **Boîte de vitesses**

Transmission avec coupleur centrifuge. 4 vitesses et une marche arrière.

- **Pont arrière**

Suspendu à double démultiplication.

- **Freins**

Frein à pied pneumatique sur les quatre roues
Frein de secours à commande pneumatique sur les roues arrière
Frein à main agissant sur le nez de pont et commandé par cylindre à ressort.

- **Equipements pneumatiques**

Compresseur sur moteur, bicylindre avec culasse à circulation d'eau; débit: 300 l/min à 2000 tr/min sous une pression de 8,5 bar.

- **Direction**

Assistée par une servo-commande hydraulique.

- **Suspension**

Mixte à l'avant (ressort et soufflet pneumatique) entièrement pneumatique à l'arrière.

- **Equipements électriques**

Alimentation en 24 V par 2 batteries de 12 V-160 Ah.

- **Roues et pneumatiques**

Roues du type à disque avec jante, équipées de pneumatiques.
La pression de gonflage est de 8,5 bar à l'avant et de 7 bar à l'arrière.

1 **A** is an 'autobus standard', a popular model with the RATP.

- **a** How many forward gears are there?
- **b** On how many wheels do the brakes operate?
- **c** How many batteries supply power?
- **d** What are the tyre pressures?

2 Extract **B** comes from literature describing 'l'autobus articulé RVI PR 180'.

- **a** How many doors would you find on a 'PR 180'?
- **b** How many passengers may board/alight at the same time?
- **c** How many passengers may be carried on 'town' buses? How many of them would have seats?
- **d** How many people are carried on route 215? How many seats are provided?

L'AUTOBUS ARTICULE RV1 PR 180

Les particularités de l'autobus articulé

L'autobus articulé RVI PR 180 comporte trois portes à deux vantaux. Ces portes ont une ouverture de 1,20 m offrant le passage simultané à deux voyageurs. Elles sont disposées de la façon suivante: la première à l'avant, la seconde à l'arrière de la caisse antérieure, la troisième en avant de l'essieu arrière.

En version urbaine, l'autobus articulé a une capacité de 127 places dont 47 assises, en majorité dans le sens de la marche. Mais dans la version rapide, destinée à la ligne 215, le nombre des places assises sera de 64—toutes dans le sens de la marche—sur un total de 116 places. Cet aménagement répond à la préoccupation d'augmenter le nombre des places assises sur des trajets relativement longs, ce qui est le cas des lignes autoroutières.

Railway travel

Signs

1 Look at these signs found on French railway stations, and answer the questions:

- **a** What information would you expect to find near sign **A**?
- **b** Where is sign **B** directing you?
- **c** What information is given in sign **C**?
- **d** What would you find at sign **D**?
- **e** What might you buy at sign **E**?
- **f** What would you hope to obtain at sign **F**?

A

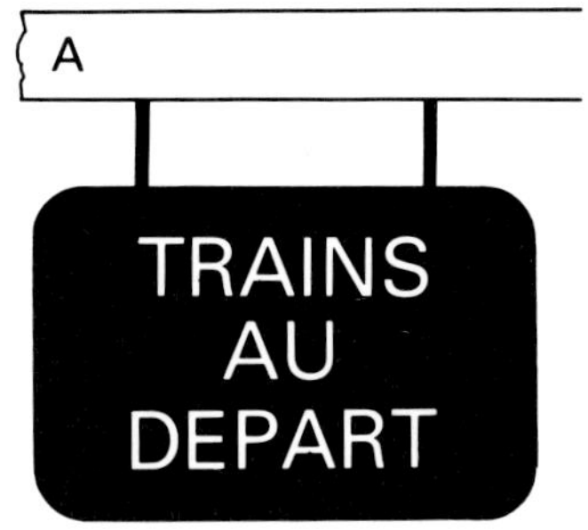

B

C

D

E

F

2 **G** shows some common signs found on French railway stations. Match them up to the words below:

Location de voitures	Chariot porte-bagages
Téléphone	Relais—toilettes
Change	Bureau de poste
Information	Salle d'attente
Location de vélos	Caféteria
Point rencontre	Consigne automatique
Objets trouvés	Restaurant
Autocars SNCF	Handicapés
Réservation	Parcotrain
Composteur	Toilettes

G

Tickets and information

1 You are in a railway station, planning trips to neighbouring towns. First you examine departure list **A**.

a You wish to visit Paris. Which would be the best train to catch, as near as possible to 6.00 am?

b How many trains leave for Lille before 7.30 am?

c State the destinations of trains leaving from platform 3 between 6.00 am and 8.00 am.

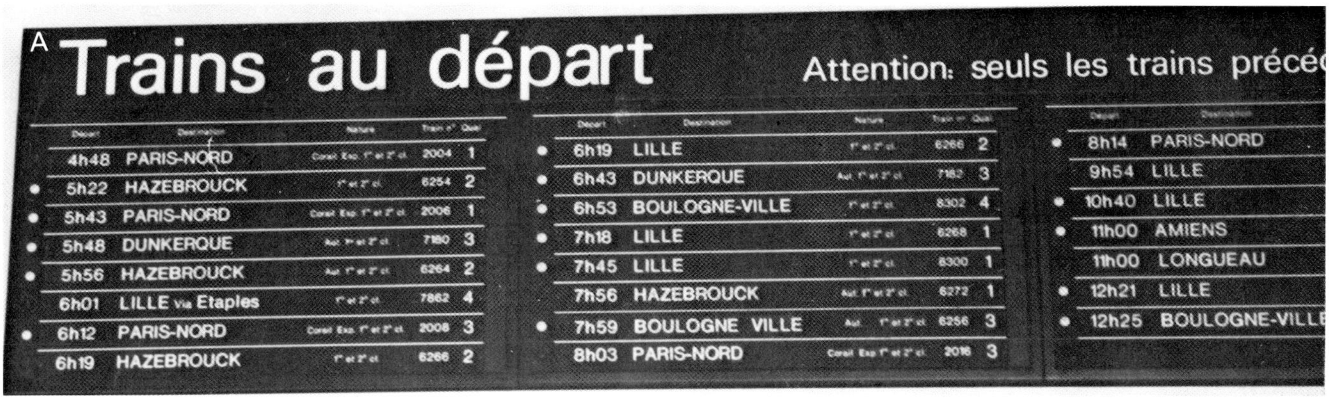

2 Machine **B** is seen frequently on railway stations. What would you purchase from it?

3 For what three different reasons would you be given tickets **C**, **D** and **E**?

C

D

E

4 On arrival in France for the start of a touring holiday you pick up leaflet **F** giving guidelines on using French trains:

a You are told that 'guichets' offer several services. Give three examples.

b Sometimes you may have to pay a supplement:
Give two instances when this is required.
When would you learn this?

c How would you recognise a date-stamping machine?

d How many berths are found in: **i** first class couchettes? **ii** second-class couchettes?

e What are you advised to do before travelling in a sleeper?

f How would you recognise staff and what is their function?

g What exactly will you find on Departure/Arrival boards?

h How would you find the exact location of your carriage?

F

Les guichets
C'est le lieu où vous pouvez acheter vos billets, obtenir des renseignements et, dans certains cas, faire des réservations ou faire annoter votre billet en cas d'arrêt en cours de route, d'abandon de parcours ou de changement d'itinéraire.

Le supplément
Certains Trans-Europ-Express, Intercités trains désignés et T.G.V. donnent lieu au paiement d'un supplément en plus du prix du billet.
Ces trains sont signalés lors de la réservation ou sur les panneaux d'affichage. Renseignez-vous avant le départ.

Le compostage
Votre billet est validé par compostage. Le composteur est ce petit appareil orange dans lequel vous devez glisser votre billet avant de prendre place dans le train.

Le train. . . la nuit

Le voyage de nuit vous permet de gagner du temps et de prolonger d'autant votre séjour et de visiter, le jour, les régions touristiques. Vous pouvez voyager en compartiment couchettes 1re classe de 4 places, ou en compartiment couchettes 2e classe de 6 places.
Le voyage en voiture-lits vous procure un plus grand confort.
Vous y trouverez plusieurs type de places dans des compartiments de 1, 2 ou 3 lits.
Il est conseillé de réserver sa place.

Les cabines 8
Dans les voitures de 2e classe de certains trains, de nouvelles banquettes (8 par compartiment) permettent, grâce à leur forme semi-allongée, un meilleur repos aux voyageurs circulant habituellement en places assises.
Ces places sont accessibles sans supplément de prix. La réservation est possible au prix habituel d'une place assise.

Les agents d'accueil et tableaux d'affichage
Dans toutes les gares des agents S.N.C.F. identifiables par leur tenue sont à votre disposition pour vous aider et vous guider. Par ailleurs, existent systématiquement des tableaux de départ et d'arrivée des trains qui vous renseigneront sur les horaires, les numéros des trains, les numéros des quais, les heures exactes. . . Enfin, dans la plupart des grandes gares et directement sur les quais concernés, vous trouverez des tableaux vous donnant la composition des trains et vous permettant de repérer l'endroit exact où votre voiture va stationner.

The Métro and RER

Signs and tariffs

1 The signs in **A** can be seen in the Métro, RER and RATP. Write down the meaning of each sign.

A

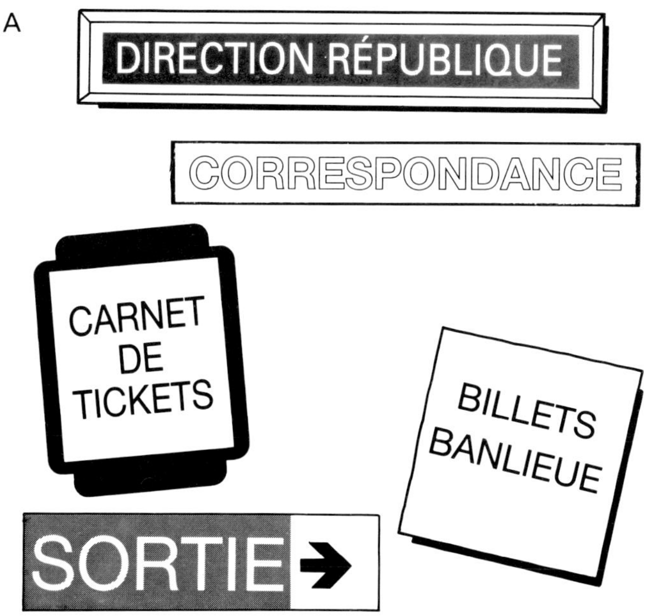

2 **B** gives some details on fares and tickets for the Métro and RER:

- **a** Does the fare on the Métro depend on the distances travelled?
- **b** Does the fare include changing to different lines?
- **c** How much would you pay for two carnets: full fare? second class?
- **d** What change would you receive from a 100 franc note if you bought: a booklet of ten first class tickets? two booklets at half price?
- **e** How much would you pay for a first-class single ticket?
- **f** What do the words Métro-Autobus tell you when they appear on second-class tickets?
- **g** How is the fare assessed on RER?

LES TARIFS DES BILLETS ET DES CARTES HEBDOMADAIRES "12 VOYAGES"

MÉTRO (lignes 1 à 13)

La tarification du métro est indépendante du parcours à effectuer. Elle permet la libre correspondance entre les lignes.

Cette tarification unique, dite urbaine, englobe la partie intra-muros, dite "section urbaine", du RER (voir plus bas).

	2e classe	1re classe
Prix du carnet de 10 billets plein tarif tarif réduit	 27,50 F 13,80 F	 42,00 F 21,00 F
Prix du billet à l'unité	4,60 F	6,80 F
Prix de la carte hebdomadaire "12 voyages" (2e classe seulement)	25,00 F	

Notez qu'il est plus économique d'acheter des billets en carnet qu'à l'unité.

Les billets de carnet de 2e classe portent la double mention "MÉTRO-AUTOBUS" car vous pouvez aussi les utiliser dans les autobus (voir plus bas).

RER (lignes A, B et C)

La tarification du RER dépend du parcours à effectuer.

La tarification urbaine du métro est appliquée sur la **"section urbaine"** du RER qui s'étend de :

- Charles-de-Gaulle-Étoile à Nation sur la ligne A (RATP),
- Gare du Nord à Gentilly sur la ligne B (RATP),
- Boulevard Victor à Boulevard Masséna sur la ligne C (SNCF).

Au-delà de la section urbaine, le RER est divisé en **"sections de banlieue"** et les prix progressent en fonction du nombre de sections parcourues jusqu'à un maximum de :

- 15,20 F et 22,90 F pour les billets à plein tarif de 2e et de 1re classe.
- 7,60 F et 11,50 F pour les billets à tarif réduit de 2e et de 1re classe.
- 72,00 F pour la carte hebdomadaire "12 voyages" (2e classe).

Ces prix correspondent au plus long parcours entre Paris (section urbaine comprise) et la banlieue (sur le RER-RATP).

Information

1 Read **A** and answer these questions:

- **a** How many routes are there in the Métro?
- **b** How many kilometres does the system cover?
- **c** How many stations are in the inner city district?
- **d** What are the number and length of: the longest route? the shortest route?
- **e** What are you told about routes in the suburbs?

A

Le métro d'aujourd'hui

● **La situation actuelle**

Le métro, dont la vocation est la desserte de Paris et de la proche banlieue comprend quinze lignes (13 lignes principales et 2 courtes lignes de rabattement), constituant un réseau aux mailles serrées de 192km:

● dans Paris intra-muros, l'ensemble des lignes atteint une longueur de 157,9km jalonnée de 315 stations.

La ligne la plus longue, y compris la partie hors Paris, est la ligne 8 avec 22km, la ligne la plus courte, la ligne 3 bis avec 1,3km, la longueur moyenne atteignant 12,8km.

● en banlieue, la longueur des lignes représente 34,3km.

10 lignes (1, 3, 5, 7, 8, 9, 10, 11, 12 et 13) sortent de Paris, la ligne ayant la plus grande longueur hors de la capitale étant la ligne 13 avec 9,3 km.

B

◀ Le confort, en particulier la douceur du roulement et de la suspension, la diminution des bruits ainsi que les performances remarquables d'accélération et de freinage auraient dû encourager la généralisation du matériel sur pneumatiques.

2 The Paris Métro features trains with pneumatic tyres. According to **B**, what three advantages do 'les trains sur pneumatiques' have?

3 Illustration **C** shows a MF77 train (on the left) and the older Sprague-Thomson model (on the right). Read the information and answer these questions:

- **a** Over what period of time were 'Sprague-Thomson' trains made?
- **b** Give one reason for their withdrawal from use.
- **c** When did the first new train run and on what route?
- **d** Give two pieces of technical data on the MF77.

C

LE 'METRO BLANC' MF 77

Une nouvelle génération de matériel roulant

Au lendemain de la seconde guerre mondiale, les voitures Sprague-Thomson, construites entre 1908 et 1938, ne répondaient plus aux normes de confort souhaitées par le public. De plus, elles n'étaient pas conçues pour recevoir les appareils de pilotage automatique.
Leur remplacement devenait un objectif prioritaire. Un matériel, appelé **matériel articulé**, fut mis au point en vue de moderniser le parc.
La première rame circula le 24 février 1952 sur la ligne 13 (Saint-Lazare/Carrefour Pleyel).
Chaque élément articulé se présentait sous la forme de trois caisses solidaires entre elles, montées sur quatre bogies (au lieu de six habituels pour un train de trois voitures). La suppression de deux bogies entraînait un gain notable de poids et, de ce fait, une économie de courant de traction.

Air travel

Timetables and information

1 **A** appears inside an airline ticket. What exactly does it mean?

A

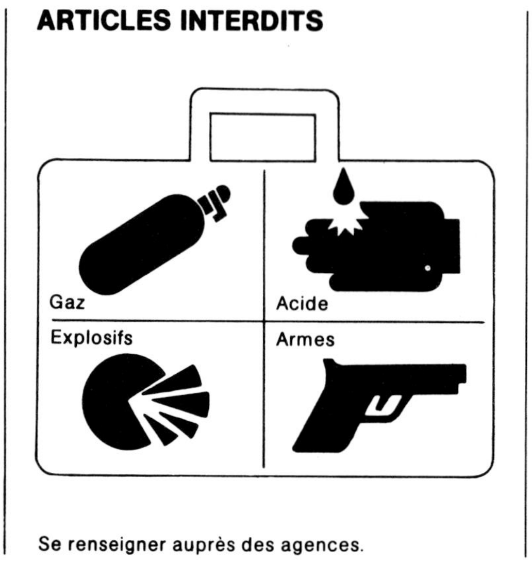

2 Look at **B**. List eight different places in the terminal building, in French and English.

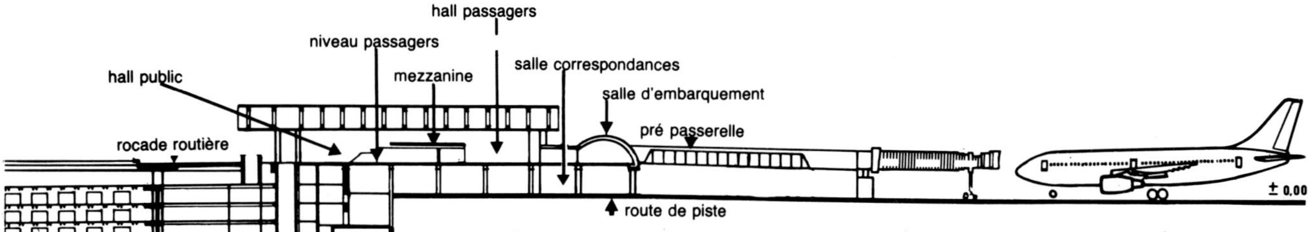

Coupe du Terminal B (Moyen-courrier)

3 **C** is an advertisement for *Air France*. Read it and answer the questions.

a When could you visit the Hotel Parker-Meridien with this *Air France* offer?

b What do they consider to be a weekend?

c How much does it cost to stay at the hotel for one night?

d If you flew by *Concorde*, how would you reach the hotel?

e What other privilege would you enjoy?

4 Timetable **D** shows *British Caledonian* flights.

a What period does this timetable cover?

b How often does flight BR 883 operate?

c When does flight BR 883 leave Paris?

d Why should weekend travellers check timetables involving Flight BR 895

e When exactly does BR 888 operate?

C

AIR FRANCE

MERIDIEN NEW YORK

OFFRE SPÉCIALE
Du 1er juin au 28 septembre 1986,
l'hôtel Parker Meridien à New York,
un des plus beaux fleurons de la chaîne,
vous offre de passer un week-end à New York
(jeudi, vendredi, samedi, dimanche)
pour 120 US D hors taxe la nuit
pour une chambre simple ou double.

SI VOUS VOYAGEZ EN CONCORDE
Du 1er septembre au 30 novembre 1986,
Air France et Parker Meridien vous offrent le transport
par limousine entre Kennedy Airport et l'hôtel.
Les meilleures chambres
sont mises à votre disposition immédiatement
Vous serez ainsi les premiers arrivés grâce à Concorde
et les premiers à pied d'œuvre à New York.

D

British Caledonian

HORAIRE VALABLE DU 12 MAI AU 25 OCTOBRE 1986
(Arrivées et départs à/de Paris 1 h plus tôt
à partir du 28 septembre 1986)

PARIS - LONDRES

Vol n°	BR 881 C/Y	BR 883 C/Y	BR 885 C/Y	BR 889 C/Y	BR 893 C/Y	BR 895 C/Y
Fréquence	QUOTIDIEN					QUOT. sauf samedi
PARIS (CDG. 1)	0800	1000	1200	1530	1730	1930
LONDRES (Gatwick)	0755	1000	1200	1530	1730	1930

LONDRES - PARIS

Vol n°	BR 882 C/Y	BR 884 C/Y	BR 886 C/Y	BR 888 C/Y	BR 892 C/Y	BR 894 C/Y	BR 896 C/Y
Fréquence	QUOT.	QUOT.	DIM.	QUOT. sauf DIM.	QUOT.	QUOT. sauf samedi	QUOTI-DIEN
LONDRES (Gatwick)	0730	0930	1100	1300	1500	1700	1930
PARIS (CDG. 1)	0925	1130	1255	1455	1655	1855	2125

Travel by sea

Signs and notices

1 Notice **A** appears on cross-Channel ships, explaining what people should do in an emergency.
   a What would you hear if there was an emergency?
   b How would messages be relayed?

2 You see notice **B** on a cross-Channel vessel. What instructions does it give drivers?

B

CHAUFFEURS:
ATTENTION

Prière de ne pas mettre votre moteur en marche avant d'avoir reçu le signal de débarquement.

3 You are crossing the Channel and see notice **C** on the ship. Match up these words with the diagram:
   a Bar
   b Cadeaux
   c Boutique hors taxes
   d Restaurant/Café
   e Change
   f Renseignements

A

SIGNAUX D'ALARME

EN CAS DE DANGER, UN SIGNAL D'ALARME REPETE SERA LANCE. QUAND CE SIGNAL SERA ENTENDU LES PASSAGERS SE RENDRONT AU POINT DE BATEAU INDIQUE PAR VOIE DE MESSAGE GENERAL (HAUT-PARLEURS) OU PAR UN MEMBRE DE L'EQUIPAGE. VOUS RECEVREZ ALORS DES CEINTURES DE SAUVETAGE ET DES INSTRUCTIONS COMPLEMENTAIRES

C

Brochures and advertisements

1 A French person is considering taking a trip to York using North Sea Ferries. Look at advertisement **A** and answer the questions:

a How long does the trip last?
b How many nights are spent on board?
c At what time could a person board in Zeebrugge and when does the vessel leave for Hull?
d Give any two details about the meal provided.
e Where would a person sleep on board and what other facility is provided?
f When does the vessel reach Hull?
g What happens after the midday meal, and at 3.30 pm?
h When does the return journey to Zeebrugge start?
i On the third day, what food and drink is on offer?

A

North Sea Ferries

Minitrips pour groupes

YORK

Minitrip 3 jours (2 nuits à bord)

(du 1er septembre 1986 au 31 mars 1987)

Programme

Premier jour :
– Traversée Zeebrugge-Hull.
– 17.00 h : embarquement à bord du Norwind ou du Norwave.
– 18.00 h : départ pour Hull.
– Dîner à bord (potage, buffet froid, repas chauds, dessert et café).
– Logement à bord en cabine standard avec lavabo.
– Soirée libre à bord (boutiques hors taxes, piste de danse).

Deuxième jour :
– Tasse de thé au réveil dans la cabine.
– Petit déjeuner anglais à bord.
– 08.30 h : arrivée à Hull et débarquement.
– 09.00 h : départ par A 1079 pour York.
– 10.15 h : arrivée à York.
– 10.30 h : visite du "Castle Museum".
– 12.00 h : "Ploughman's lunch" chez Oscar's (Little Stonegate).
– Temps libre pour faire votre shopping.
– 15.30 h : départ de York, par Market Weighton, South Cave et le Humber Bridge vers Hull.
– 17.00 h : arrivée à Hull King George Dock et embarquement.
– 18.00 h : départ du navire vers Zeebrugge.
– Dîner et logement (voir premier jour).

Troisième jour :
– Tasse de thé au réveil dans la cabine.
– Petit déjeuner anglais à bord.
– 09.00 h : arrivée et débarquement à Zeebrugge.

2 **B** gives details of a popular cross-Channel service.

- **a** How many vessels operate on this service?
- **b** How many sailings are there in each direction?
- **c** How long is the Calais–Dover crossing?
- **d** What roads take you from Calais to Paris and how long would this journey take?
- **e** If you own a car how long before sailing do you have to report?

3 A French family is considering visiting England. They examine brochure **C**.

- **a** How much would one day in Dover cost for two adults and a child?
- **b** Name two attractions offered in the 60-hour visit to Kent.
- **c** If a French person decides to go on the 120-hour trip, what three things is she likely to see?

SEALINK EN VOITURE POUR L'ANGLETERRE L'ANGLETERRE EN VOITURE

Calais–Douvres

4 car-ferries géants, ultra-modernes, hyper-confortables, assurent une navette toute l'année, toute la journée. Ils sont tellement agréables qu'on les prendrait tous les jours.

Calais–Douvres, c'est la ligne continue.
4 car-ferries géants
—*Champs-Elysées* (Sealink SNCF)
—*Côte d'Azur* (Sealink SNCF)
—*St Anselm* (Sealink British Ferries)
—*St Christopher* (Sealink British Ferries)

- Jusqu'à 16 départs dans chaque sens.
- La nuit comme le jour.
- Accès et embarquement faciles.

L'autoroute A1 puis la A26 jusqu'à son terminus actuel, ensuite la RN43, mettent le terminal SEALINK à environ 3h de Paris.

Durée de la traversée: 1 h 30.

Délai de présentation:
30mn avant le départ.

B

C

Douvres et le Kent

Un jour à Douvres

Douvres a su marier à la fois l'intérêt touristique et le plaisir d'un vrai shopping. Visitez le château et la maison romaine, faites une promenade sur le front de mer ou découvrez les bonnes affaires de ses nombreux commerces.

Traversée maritime
aller/retour
ENFANT : 76 F.

110

60 heures dans le Kent

Jardin de l'Angleterre, le Kent au printemps ou en été vous offre ses paysages verdoyants, ses cottages typiques, sa douceur de vivre et ses villes animées.

Traversées maritimes
aller/retour
ENFANT : 96 F.

192

120 heures en Angleterre

L'idéal pour voir le maximum de choses et profiter de l'Angleterre. La côte et ses stations balnéaires vous proposent détente et amusement. Les châteaux, jardins et vestiges du temps passé attendent votre visite. Et pour l'ambiance, les pubs sont là.

Traversées maritimes
aller/retour
ENFANT : 126 F

252

4 D shows examples of vessels found in the *Brittany Ferries* fleet:

- **a** Which ships have been modernised?
- **b** Which is: the heaviest? the longest? the fastest?
- **c** Which vessel carries:
  the smallest number of crew members?
  the smallest number of cabins?
  the fewest reclining seats?
- **d** Which ship has the greatest restaurant seating capacity?
- **e** Are facilities for children provided on all the vessels?
- **f** Name two facilities that are not provided on *Tregastel* which are found on the other two ships.

D

QUIBERON

CONSTRUCTION	1975. RENOVATION 1982
JAUGE	8313 TONNEAUX
LONGUEUR	129 METRES
LARGEUR	21 METRES
VITESSE	21 NOEUDS
PROPULSION	4 MOTEURS DE 4000 CH.
ENERGIE ELECTRIQUE FOURNIE PAR	3 MOTEURS DE 1165 CH.
CAPACITE PASSAGERS	1143 PASSAGERS
MEMBRE D'EQUIPAGE	80
NOMBRE DE CABINES	207
NOMBRE DE COUCHETTES	686
NOMBRE DE SIEGES INCLINABLES	76
STABILISATEUR ANTI-ROULIS	OUI
RESTAURANT - 250 PLACES	1
CAFETERIA-CROISSANTERIE - 250 PLACES	1
BAR	1
BOUTIQUES HORS TAXES	2
SALLE DE JEUX ENFANTS	1
CINEMA	1
CIRCUIT VIDEO	OUI
ASCENSEUR	OUI
NOMBRE DE VOITURES	260
LIGNES EFFECTUÉES	ROSCOFF/PLYMOUTH ROSCOFF/CORK PLYMOUTH/SANTANDER

ARMORIQUE

CONSTRUCTION	1972 RENOVATION 1979
JAUGE	5731 TONNEAUX
LONGUEUR	116,65 METRES
LARGEUR	19,20 METRES
VITESSE	19 NOEUDS
PROPULSION	2 MOTEURS DE 6000 CH.
ENERGIE ELECTRIQUE FOURNIE PAR	3 MOTEURS DE 850 CH.
STABILISATEUR ANTI-ROULIS	OUI
CAPACITE PASSAGERS	700
MEMBRE D'EQUIPAGE	60
NOMBRE DE CABINES	188
NOMBRE DE COUCHETTES	408
NOMBRE DE SIEGES INCLINABLES	244
NOMBRE DE VOITURES	160
RESTAURANT - 87 PLACES	1
CAFETERIA-CROISSANTERIE - 138 PLACES	1
BAR	2
CINEMA	1
SALLE DE JEUX ENFANTS	1
BOUTIQUES HORS TAXES	2
CIRCUIT VIDEO	OUI
ASCENSEUR	2
LIGNES EFFECTUÉES	ST MALO/PORSMOUTH

TREGASTEL

CONSTRUCTION	1971
JAUGE	3999 TONNEAUX
LONGUEUR	118 METRES
LARGEUR	18,50 METRES
VITESSE	18 NOEUDS
PROPULSION	2 MOTEURS DE 6700 CV.
ENERGIE ELECTRIQUE FOURNIE PAR	3 MOTEURS DE 1150 CV.
CAPACITE PASSAGERS	1200 PASSAGERS
MEMBRE D'EQUIPAGE	70
NOMBRE DE CABINES	83
NOMBRE DE COUCHETTES	248
NOMBRE DE SIEGES INCLINABLES	400
NOMBRE DE VOITURES	340
RESTAURANT - 160 PLACES	1
COFFEE SHOP - 291 PLACES	1
BAR	1
BOUTIQUES HORS TAXES	2
SALLE DE JEUX ENFANTS	1
ASCENSEUR	1
LIGNES EFFECTUÉES	ROSCOFF/PLYMOUTH ROSCOFF/CORK

The Tourist Office

Signs, notice and advertisements

1 You have just arrived in a French town and want to find out more about the area. **A** shows some of the signs and notices displayed in the Tourist Office. Match up the words below with the illustrations.

villages de vacances
locations de caravanes et de camping-cars
le chemin de fer
par mer
locations de vacances en espace rural
camping
l'autocar
l'avion
locations de vélos et mobylettes
par air
spéléologie
l'artisanat
promenades en mer
tourisme équestre
aéroclubs et parachutisme
archéologie
mini-golf
karting
stades de neige
les sources thermales
la chasse
la pêche en rivière
circuits pédestres

A

2 You have just arrived at Tourist Office **B** but find it closed.

a How long is the lunch break?
b When does the office close in the evenings?

3 **C** shows notices on the door of a Syndicat d'Initiative.

a On what date is the office closed and at what time?
b How would you attract a member of staff's attention if the door were locked?

Tourist information

1 **A** advertises a Tourist Office.

a Where is La Côte d'Azur?
b What sort of information will Le Bureau d'Accueil give you?
c Who would be likely to help you at the Esplanade du Paillon?
d State exactly what information the Esplanade du Paillon can give you?

A

BUREAU D'ACCUEIL
TOURISME COTE D'AZUR
A
NICE

tous les renseignements sur:
* l'hébergement,
* les loisirs,
* les manifestations,
* les sports,

sont disponibles au BUREAU D'ACCUEIL

TOURISME COTE D'AZUR
GARE ROUTIERE DE NICE

Esplanade du Paillon
Téléphone 93.80.84.84

où des hôtesses sont à votre disposition pour vous conseiller sur:

— les randonnées pédestres,
— les circuits routiers,
— les sites et curiosités des Alpes-Maritimes,
— les suggestions d'itinéraires selon vos préférences (mer, montagne, campagne, patrimoine, etc. . .)

2 Look at notice **B**.

  a When is the season for Bordeaux and Caen?

  b What are the hours of opening on Sundays at Caen?

  c What are the exact times of opening out of season at Bordeaux?

3 On holiday in the south of France you call in at the Tourist Office and obtain maps **C** and **D** showing the port areas of Nice and Toulon.

  a In French, direct a passer-by from the Gare Maritime in Toulon to la Gare SNCF.

  b Give directions on how to reach the Quai Cassini from Promenade des Anglais in Nice.

C

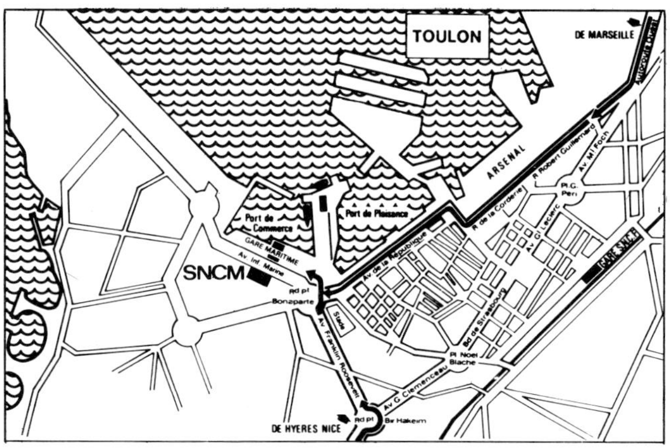

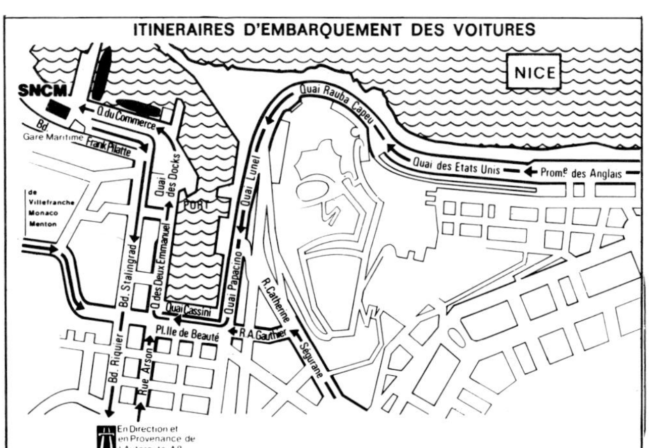

D

BORDEAUX

ACCUEIL D'AQUITAINE

Départements de Dordogne / Gironde / Landes / Lot-et-Garonne Pyrénées-Atlantiques

OFFICE DE TOURISME / SYNDICAT D'INITIATIVE

12, COURS DU 30 JUILLET 33080 BORDEAUX CEDEX

☎ 56.44.28.41 / Tx 570 362 ACCUEIL BX

Heures d'ouverture:

Saison: 1er Juin au 31 Août

9 h-19 h du Lundi au Samedi / 9 h-14 h le Dimanche

Hors saison: 9 h-12 h 15 et 13 h 45-18 h 30 du Lundi au Samedi

CAEN

ACCUEIL DE NORMANDIE

Départements du Calvados / Manche / Orne

OFFICE DE TOURISME / SYNDICAT D'INITIATIVE

PLACE SAINT-PIERRE 14300 CAEN

☎ 31.86.27.65 / Tx 170 353

Heures d'ouverture:

Saison: Juillet - Août

8 h 45-19 h 30 du Lundi au Samedi / 10 h-12 h et 14 h-17 h le Dimanche

Hors saison: 8 h 45-12 h 15 et 14 h-19 h du Lundi au Samedi

B

At the customs

1 On arrival in France with friends you see notices **A–E** in the customs area. What does each of them mean?

A

B

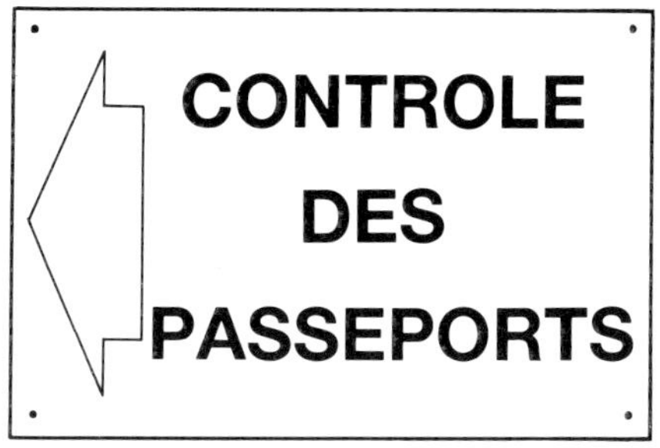

C

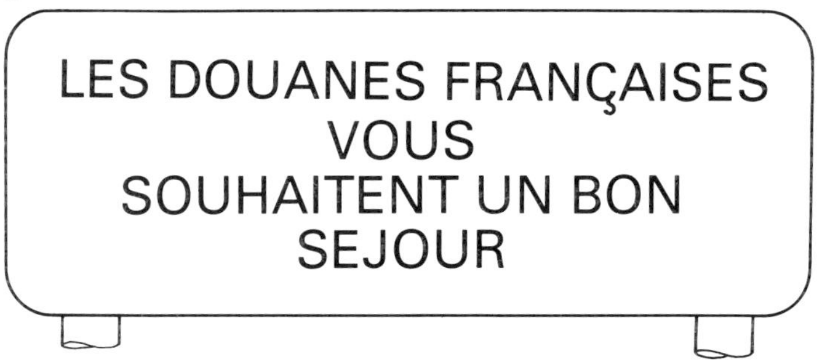

D

E

2 What age are the animals referred to in extract **F**, from a French customs poster?

F

L'entrée en France des animaux de moins de 3 ans est interdite. Pour ceux de plus de 3 ans elle est limitée à trois animaux dont un seul chiot

3 According to **G** what is the condition of entry for animals arriving in the Channel Isles and mainland Britain?

G

Chats, chiens et autres mammifères ne peuvent entrer dans les îles Britanniques et Anglo-Normandes qu'après six mois de quarantaine

4 Look at **H**.

- **a** What age is mentioned in this Customs document?
- **b** What amount of alcohol can a French person buy on this journey?
- **c** How much perfume and toilet water may be purchased?

H

Faites vos achats hors taxes. A partir de dix-sept ans, les Français peuvent profiter des tolérances douanières à bord et voici tout ce que vous pourrez rapporter avec vous en France: 300 cigarettes ou 150 cigarillos ou 75 cigares ou 400 g de tabac, 1 litre d'alcool de plus de 22° ou 3 litres d'alcool de moins de 22°, 4 litres de vin, 75 g de parfum et 3/8 de litre d'eau de toilette.

Banking

Signs and currency

1 Where would you expect to find poster **A**?
2 You are on holiday in France and run out of money on a Sunday. Why would sign **B** be a welcome sight?

B

3 While staying with a French pen-friend in Paris you buy some souvenirs before leaving for home. They come to 85 francs. What change would you expect from the notes in **C**?

C

A

4 You receive the change shown in **D** in a French shop. How much have you been given?

D

In the bank

1 You go into a French bank to change money. Work out the English for these comments made by the bank clerk:

- **a** Vous avez votre passeport?
- **b** Aujourd'hui, la livre est à 10 francs 30.
- **c** Signez là, s'il vous plaît.
- **d** Allez là-bas, Madame, au 'Change'

2 Banking hours vary in France, but as a general rule banks are open from 8.30 am or 9.00 am until 4.00 pm or 5.00 pm. Which of the responses best describes closing time:

- **a** à onze heures.
- **b** à quatorze heures.
- **c** à seize heures.

3 Match up the English sentences on the left with the ones in French in the right-hand column.

A person asks the way to the bank.	A combien est la livre aujourd'hui?
On arrival he asks what he must do in order to cash traveller's cheques.	Pardon, Monsieur, où se trouve la banque?
He produces four documents as a means to identification.	Pour changer un chèque de voyage, c'est à quel guichet, s'il vous plaît?
He then enquires about the rate of exchange.	Est-ce que je peux faire un emprunt à long terme?
He then asks about a long term loan.	Est-ce qu'il est possible de faire virer mon salaire directement sur compte?
He makes enquiries about having his salary paid into his bank account.	Que vous faut-il? J'ai mon passeport, ma carte d'identité, mon permis de conduire, ma carte d'étudiant.

4 You work in a French bank, what do you say or give to customers who ask the following:

- **a** Est-ce que vous pouvez me changer ces chèques de voyage?
- **b** Est-ce que vous pouvez me donner des pièces de 10 francs s'il vous plaît?
- **c** Donnez-moi trois billets et de la monnaie s'il vous plaît.
- **d** Quel est le cours du change?
- **e** Quelle commission prenez-vous?

Food and drink

Signs and menus

1 Walking along a French street you see notice **A** in a window. What is on sale here?

2 What items on **B** can you buy for 30 francs?

B

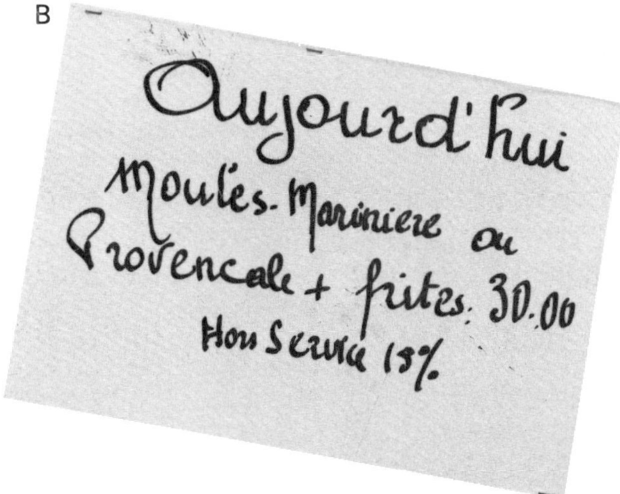

3 Your friend likes sea food and stops to look at the restaurant display in **C**. See if you can answer his questions:

- **a** When is the shop open?
- **b** Can you buy oysters here?
- **c** Are lobsters available?
- **d** What is a 'vignot'?
- **e** Would you be able to buy shrimps and prawns here?

4 While staying in France you notice **D**, a fascinating café specialising in different sorts of tea. What do the following mean:
thé à la cérise
thé au citron
thé à la fraise
thé au miel
thé à la pistache
thé à la pomme
thé vert menthe?

5 Strolling down a French road your attention is drawn to sign **E** outside a baker's shop. Which *five* items are on sale?

E

6 You spot menu **F** outside a French café:
   a How many fish dishes are available?
   b What is the difference between the two types of omelette?
   c With which dish would you commence a meal, and how much would it cost?

F

Café Merville

Poulet et frites	38
Steak et frites	42
Filet de Boeuf	64
Fondue	11
Beignets de poisson	35
Moules	30
Omelette nature	22
Omelette variée	28
Oeufs Bacon	30
Saucisses et frites	29
Soupe du jour	13

D

7 Having explored a French town you decide to have a rest and a drink. You see the café sign shown in **G**.
   a How do you know that reading material would be available?
   b What else can be bought here?

G

8 Look at sign **H**.

a In French, give details of how you would reach the restaurant.

b What two commodities are offered here, in addition to restaurant facilities?

9 During a visit to France your family decides to try a meal in restaurant **I**. Since you are the only one who understands French you answer these questions from your Dad:

a How much would a meal for three people cost?

b Is there a choice of starters?

c What two things does the restaurant say about the six courses on offer?

11 You are having dinner with a friend at restaurant **K**, 'Chez Paul':

a This restaurant offers a special treat for customers ordering dinner, what is it?

b Name three sorts of food in which this restaurant specialises.

K

CHEZ PAUL

Dîners aux chandelles
Menus 80F et 100F + carte

Poissons fins-viandes-volailles
Tél 31 46 38 84

12 Travelling across France you have to change trains. While waiting for a connection you decide to have a snack at café **L**:

a Can you say what two types of food are on sale at the 'Café de la Gare'?

b When exactly is it open?

H

10 The 54-franc menu in **J** looks quite interesting:

a What do you understand by 'Autour d'un Plat'?

b Can you say what is meant by 'Rillettes de Lapin'?

c What type of pâté is served here?

J

Autour d'un Plat
54F
Rillettes de Lapin
Salade printanière au Toast de Chevre chaud
Salade folle aux Mignardises
Bagatelle de Crevettes en Coquille d'Ananas
Terrine de Poissons et son Coulis de Tomates
Aujourd'hui

L

Cafe de La Gare

ROTISSERIE
FRUITS DE MER

Tous les jours de l'année
jusqu'à 3h. du matin

31,bd. du Temple, Strasbourg

13 Following a busy day on the beach with your family you look for somewhere to eat in the evening and come across notice **M**:

  a Is service charge included in the cost of a meal?
  b Name two meat dishes on offer.
  c Describe the quantity and type of drink available.

14 On a school trip to France your party visits a restaurant. Give the French for these items you and your friends order:
vegetable soup
tomato salad
bacon and eggs
cheese omelette
roast chicken
stew
mussels
frogs' legs
boiled potatoes
chips
toasted ham and cheese sandwich

Restaurants

1 You are looking for somewhere to have a meal and find advertisements **A**, **B** and **C** in your guide book.

  a If you visited *Taverne Kronenbourg* what food would you expect to find and what sort of entertainment would be laid on?
  b Where is *Ruc L'Univers* situated and in what sort of food does it specialise?
  c For whom is *Ruc L'Univers* especially useful, and until what time does it stay open?
  d When is *L'Auberge d'Alsace* open? Where is it located? What three sorts of food does it serve?

C

2 You are enjoying the sights in Paris and your parents decide to have a meal in a restaurant. Guide **D** contains a great deal of information. Read it carefully and answer these questions:

- **a** How might you reach *Le Chalet des Iles*?
- **b** What is a speciality at *Le Corsaire* and when is this restaurant closed?
- **c** How many people could be accommodated at *Les Jardins de Bagatelle*?
- **d** State three things *Le Petit Boileau* offers.
- **e** When exactly is the *Bistro Romain* open?
- **f** What might you do on a summer visit to *Piscine Molitor* in addition to eating?
- **g** What sort of food is served at *Le Palais du Trocadéro* and why would you imagine it to be good?
- **h** When does *L'Auberge Dab* close and what are two of its specialities?
- **i** Give the opening times for *Bistro Romain* and two special features of this restaurant.
- **j** In the *Club Méditerranée* what costs: 130F? 195F? 210F?

D

liste des restaurants

BOIS DE BOULOGNE - PONT DE SEVRES - PORTE DE SAINT-CLOUD

LE CHALET DES ILES (Bois de Boulogne), le charme d'un cadre de verdure. Une bonne table à des prix raisonnables. Traversée en bateau - Déj. et dîner t.l.j. Réservation : 42.88.04.69.

LE CORSAIRE (c), 1, bd Exelmans (angle quai Louis-Blériot), 45.25.53.25 et 45.20.87.85. Carte de spéc. franco-italienne de qualité. Menu prix fixe s.c. Ouvert sam. et fermé dim. Le soir, on peut recevoir les groupes.

L'ENTRECOTE BOULOGNE, 103, bd J.-Jaurès.

LES JARDINS DE BAGATELLE (a), Parc de Bagatelle, bois de Boulogne (16ᵉ). Route de Sèvres à Neuilly (côté Seine), 47.22.88.29. Tlj midi et soir : séminaires, réceptions. Salons de 10 à 200 couverts. Menu 160 F s.c.

LE PETIT BOILEAU, 98, rue Boileau (16ᵉ), 42.88.59.05. Cuisine familiale. Produits frais. Viande excellente. Fermé dim. et sam. soir.

PASSY - AUTEUIL - TROCADERO

BELLE CHINE (c), 29, r. Copernic, Tél. : 45.00.62.19. Mº Victor-Hugo. Spéc. chinoises raffinées. Ambiance calme et typique.

BISTRO ROMAIN (c), pl. Victor-Hugo. Menu 39,90 F et 52,50 F. Nouveau : à la carte et 32 desserts. T.l.j. 11h30-15h et 18h-1h. Non stop sam. et dim..

ILE DE KASHMIR, quai Debilly - Face au 32, av. de New York. 47.23.77.78 et 47.23.50.97. Parking tous les jours, déj. et dîners à bord d'une péniche.

PISCINE MOLITOR, 6, av. Porte Molitor (16ᵉ), (Mº Michel-Ange-Molitor), 46.51.84.34. Au bord de l'eau restaurant grill, piscine d'été. Ouvert tous les jours de 9h à 22h.

PALAIS DU TROCADERO, 7, avenue d'Eylau, place du Trocadéro, 47.27.05.02. Restaurant chinois recommandé par tous les guides gastronomiques.

STELLA (c), 133, av. Victor-Hugo (16ᵉ), 47.27.60.54. Huîtres. Cuisine familiale et bourgeoise. Ouvert tous les jours jusqu'à 2h du matin.

NEUILLY-PORTE MAILLOT

AUBERGE DAB (b), 161, Av. Malakoff (16ᵉ), 45.00.32.22 et 36.57. T.l.j. jusqu'à 2h du matin. Spécialités fruits de mer, poissons, rôtisserie, choucroute.

BISTRO ROMAIN, 199, avenue Charles-de-Gaulle - Neuilly s/Seine. Menu 39,90 et 52,50 F. Carte, spécialités italiennes et 34 desserts. Matin et soir jusqu'à 1h du matin.

CLUB MEDITERRANEE (a), 58, bd Victor-Hugo, Neuilly-s-Seine, 47.58.11.00. Tlj. Sce jsq 22h30. La formule du club, avec ses grands buffets. Déjeuners 130 F et 169 F, vin et s.c. le soir et le dimanche midi 195 F et le jeudi, dîner aux chandelles avec orchestre 210 F. t.c.

Drinks

1 **A** is the price list of drinks in a restaurant.
- **a** How many non-alcoholic drinks are on sale?
- **b** What would you pay for a Pernod?
- **c** What is meant by 'infusion'?
- **d** What exactly would you receive if you asked for 'une demie d'Evian'?
- **e** Give the price for two brandies.
- **f** How much would you pay for a beer and what quantity would you receive?

2 **B** is a list of 'apéritifs' and 'digestifs' available at this high-class restaurant:
- **a** What food is available?
- **b** How much would you pay if you did not have champagne?
- **c** What would you receive for a 60-franc supplement?
- **d** Find the price of one non-alcoholic drink and say what it is.
- **e** What do you understand by the word 'digestifs'?
- **f** Is a service charge included?

PRIX APERITIFS ET DIGESTIFS

Cocktail 1 heure

Bar complet

Biscuits salés, Olives, Chips...
Whisky, Bourbon, Vodka, Bière, Martini, Gini
Jus de Tomates et d'Oranges etc...

Sans Champagne	130 FF
Avec Champagne	160 FF

Supplément Canapés Chauds et Froids:

5 pièces (3 froids, 2 chauds)	35 FF
7 pièces (4 froids, 2 chauds, 1 sucré)	60 FF
14 pièces (8 froids, 4 chauds, 2 sucrés)	90 FF

Aperitifs d'acceuil

Kir	20 FF
Kir Royal	40 FF
Punch aux Fruits	30 FF
Jus d'Oranges Frais	20FF

Digestifs

Entre 35 FF et 55 FF selon choix du client.

PRIX NETS, PAR PERSONNE, TAXES ET SERVICE 15% INCLUS.

B

KIR ROYAL : 11.10

APÉRITIFS (5 cl)

Kir			8.90
Américano			8.90
Porto « Quinta do Noval »			8.90
Martini - Byrrh - Cinzano - Raphaël - Dubonnet			8.90
Ambassadeur - Suze			8.90
Pastis 51 - Pernod - Ricard (2 cl)			8.90
Whisky White Mac Kay (4 cl)	11.20	Baby (2 cl)	5.60

Infusion	3.30	Thé	3.30
Café express	3.30		

EAUX MINÉRALES

Vittel	la demie	5.60
Badoit	la demie	5.60
Évian	la demie	5.60
Vichy Saint-Yorre	la demie	5.60

ALCOOLS ET LIQUEURS (2 cl)

Crème de cassis	8.90
BÉNÉDICTINE	8.90
Rhum	8.90
Marc de Bourgogne	8.90
Calvados	8.90
Kirsch pur	8.90
Cognac	8.90
Marie-Brizard sec	8.90
Cointreau	8.90
Grog au rhum	8.90
Mirabelle	8.90

Kronenbourg	la bouteille 25 cl	5.60
Bière export	la bouteille 33 cl	5.60
Cidre	la bouteille 33 cl	5.60

Coca-cola	6.10

A

3 Look carefully at description **C** of a champagne label, and write in English what you understand by numbers 1 to 6.

C

Dernière touche avant de laisser le Champagne répandre le bonheur partout où on l'appelle : la pose de l'étiquette qui signe son authenticité.

* * *

Cette étiquette comporte obligatoirement :

- l'appellation "Champagne" en caractères très apparents, (1)
- le nom de la marque ou de l'expéditeur, (2)
- le numéro d'immatriculation délivré par le Comité Interprofessionnel du Vin de Champagne, précédé d'initiales qui renseignent sur le producteur, (3)
- la contenance de la bouteille. (4)

Les autres mentions qui peuvent éventuellement figurer ne sont là que pour apporter des précisions, entre autres :

- l'indication du lieu où est situé l'établissement commercial ou de production, (5)
- le millésime, s'il y a lieu,
- les particularités de la cuvée, telles "blanc de blancs" ou "rosé",
- la teneur en sucre, soit, en ordre croissant, "brut", "extra-dry", "sec", "demi-sec". (6)

Shops and markets

Everyday shopping

1 Which of the following items would *not* be on sale at shop **A**?

côtelettes	saucisses
cassis	miel
langue	contre-filet
mûres	poivre
carré d'agneau	tournedos
confiture	cacahuètes

A

B

2 Walking down a French road you see shop **B**. In what sort of meat does it specialise?
3 Look at the shop window on the right in **C**. Name one item on sale.
4 What does the sign above the door in **D** mean?

C

D

5 You stop next to sign **E**. Are you outside:

a a dry cleaner's
b a dress shop
c a hardware shop
d a bookshop?

6 Which of these items could you buy at shop **F**:

un livre	un tapis
une ampoule	un sèche-cheveux
un crayon	un abat-jour
un magnétoscope	

7 In French, list six things you might find on sale in shop **G**.

8 Walking down a French road with an English friend you come to shop **H**. Explain to your friend the difference between 'une boulangerie' and 'une pâtisserie'.

I

9 Which of the following conversations might you hear in shop **I**:

- **a** Je voudrais toucher ce chèque de voyage.
- **b** Est-ce que vous pouvez préparer cette ordonnance?
- **c** Avez-vous des disques?
- **d** Avez-vous des livres en français?
- **e** Est-ce que vous avez de l'huile solaire?
- **f** Je voudrais une poêle.
- **g** Combien de fois par jour faut-il le prendre?

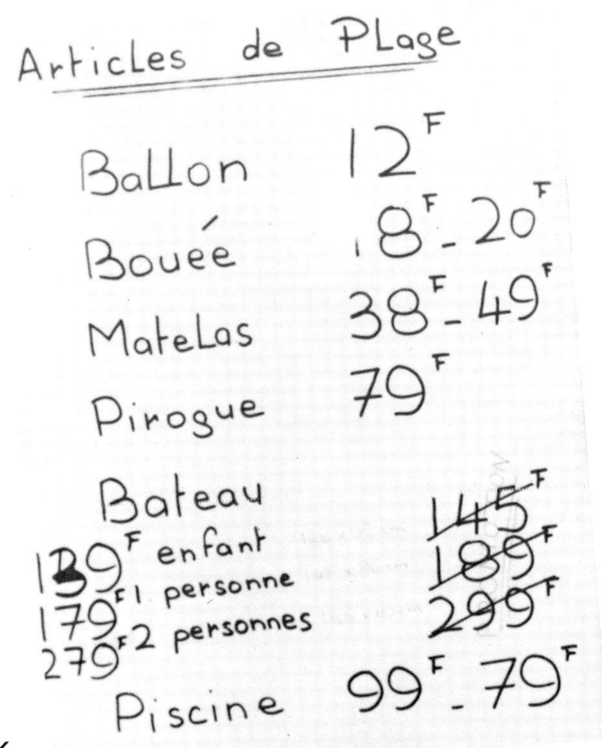

K

10 Look at **J**. What do you understand by: 'soldes'? 'Remise 20%'?

J

11 It is a hot day, ideal for beach games. You look in shop **K** for some things to use on the beach.

- **a** How much change would you receive from a 50 franc note if you bought two footballs?
- **b** What is the price of the cheapest air bed?
- **c** By how much has a two-person rubber boat been reduced?
- **d** How would you use a 'bouée'?
- **e** If you bought the most expensive paddling pool for your younger brother, how much change would you get from 100 francs?

12 Notice **L** is an advertisement for a shop.

- **a** Do you think the shop is near the coast? Why?
- **b** Where is it possible to buy the products being advertised?
- **c** What is the meaning of:
  vannerie
  ménager
  outillages
  faillites
  articles d'importation du monde entier

Signs inside shops

1. What goods would you expect to be on sale near sign **A** in a French shop?
2. What instruction is given in **B**?
3. Look at **C**. Why is school equipment being advertised at this time?

4 Sign **D** appears over a food counter.
   a What is on sale here?
   b What is the price of butter?
   c How much would one kilo of 'Fromage Le Divin Forza' cost?

5 **E** is a sign above a meat counter
   a What two sorts of meat are on sale?
   b What would the cheapest buy be and how much would 3 kilograms cost?
   c What do the expressions 'sans os' and 'avec os' mean?

6 What do you understand by the expression 'peau douce' in **F**?

7 You are staying for a month with a French family and decide to treat your hosts to some wine. You see notice **G** in a shop window.
   a Describe two qualities of the advertised wine.
   b Why is there an extra charge on each litre?

D

E

F

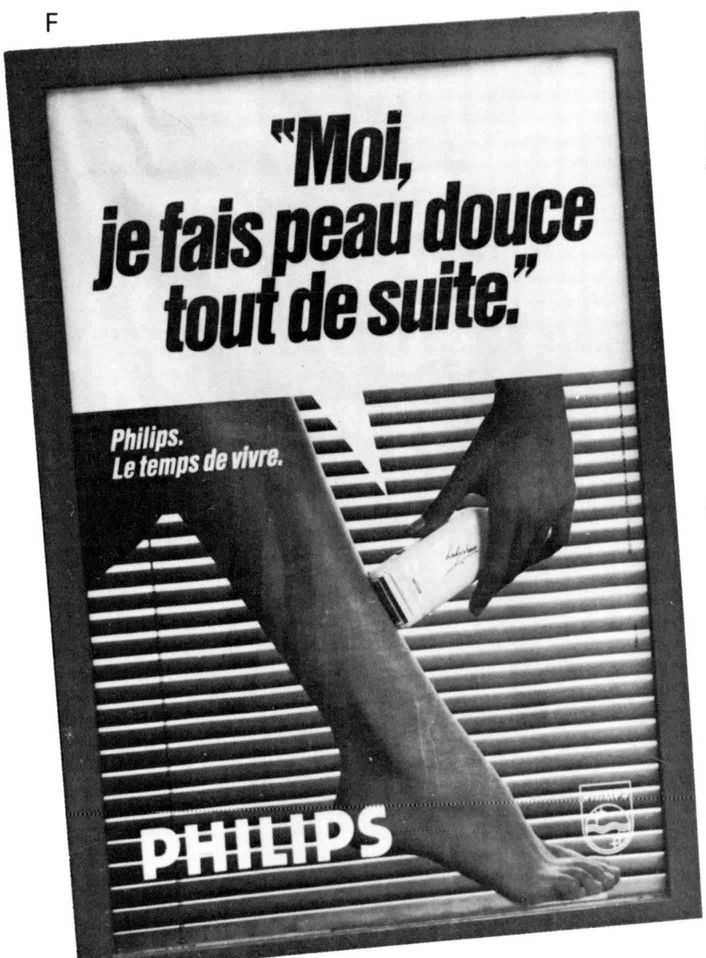

G

Bookshops, stationers, newsagents

1 You decide to browse in shop **A**. Which of these might you find inside:

un cahier	une carte-postale
de l'encre	une demi-douzaine d'oeufs
un petit pain	*Paris-Match*
Nice-Matin	des crudités
un calendrier	

2 Where would you expect to find door **B**:

a une librairie
b une papeterie
c une charcuterie
d une bibliothèque?

3 Your French penfriend is showing you around her town and you stop opposite shop **C**. 'What is that shop called in English?' she asks. What would you answer?

4 Which of the following conversations might you hear in shop **D**:

a Où puis-je acheter un journal allemand?
b Est-ce que vous vendez des ouvre-boîtes?
c Je voudrais acheter un stylo à bille.
d Est-ce que vous avez *Le Monde*?
e Est-ce que vous avez un plan de la ville?
f J'ai besoin d'une chemise.
g Je voudrais une marmite.
h Je voudrais une revue anglaise.

D

Services

1 For what reason would you go to **A**?
2 You wish to make an appointment at **B**. Which of the following phrases would you use:

a Pourriez-vous me rafraîchir?
b C'est bien, merci.
c Je voudrais fixer un rendez-vous s'il vous plaît.

A

B

3 What does sign **C** mean and where would you find it?

4 You might hear the following comments in shop **D**. What does each of them mean:
  a Je voudrais un shampooing pour cheveux gras.
  b Je voudrais les cheveux coupés.
  c Coupez-en davantage derrière.

5 Your hotel faces shop **E** and your Mum asks you about it:
  a What could you tell her about the water?
  b Explain 'Lavage-rinçage' to her.
  c What sort of machines are mentioned?
  d What service is advertised in the right-hand window?

6 As well as selling property, estate agent **F** offers two other services. What are they?

7 Sign **G** appears in an estate agent's window. Give details about the property priced at: 150,000 francs; 120,000 francs.

8 You meet the owner of van **H** in a café and begin to talk about his work. In French, give his reply to these questions:
   a Où habitez-vous?
   b Quel est votre métier?
   c Avez-vous une voiture? Comment est-elle?
   d Comment s'appelle votre magasin?

F

G
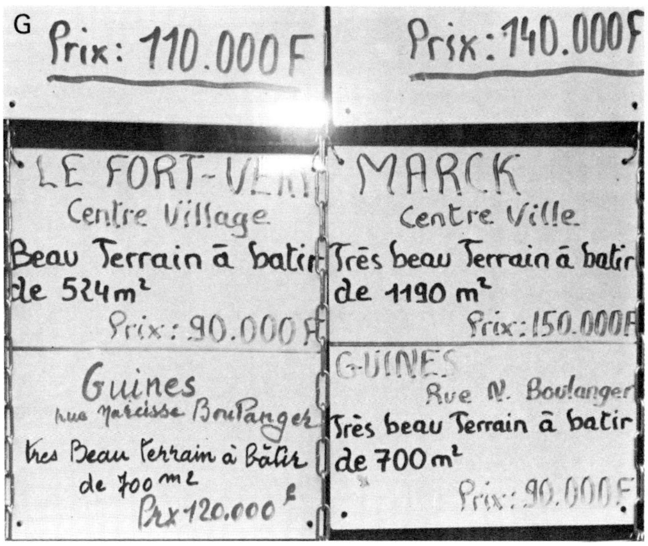

H

9 Look at window **I**.
   a What sort of business is this?
   b When is it open at the weekend?
   c State five services it offers.

I

10 The signs in **J** are in an optician's window.

a How long would you have to wait for a pair of spectacles?

b Which of the three squares in the middle of the display is best described by the following: 'Si l'on casse un verre à ses lunettes, il est inutile d'en changer la monture.'

11 Name three facilities offered to dogs in **K**.

J

K

L

12 What sort of person would come to **L**?

13 Name one occupation likely to be found in **M**.

M

14 With what place would you associate sign **N**?

N

15 Look at machine **O**.
- **a** What would you buy here?
- **b** What type of coins could you use?
- **c** What would you expect to find in the tray at the bottom right-hand side?

16 For what reason are the offices in **P** closed?

17 According to sign **Q**, what happens between 15 July and 29 August?

18 What is likely to occur if you try to open door **R**?

19 Notice **S** appears on a shop door. Can you translate it?

O

P

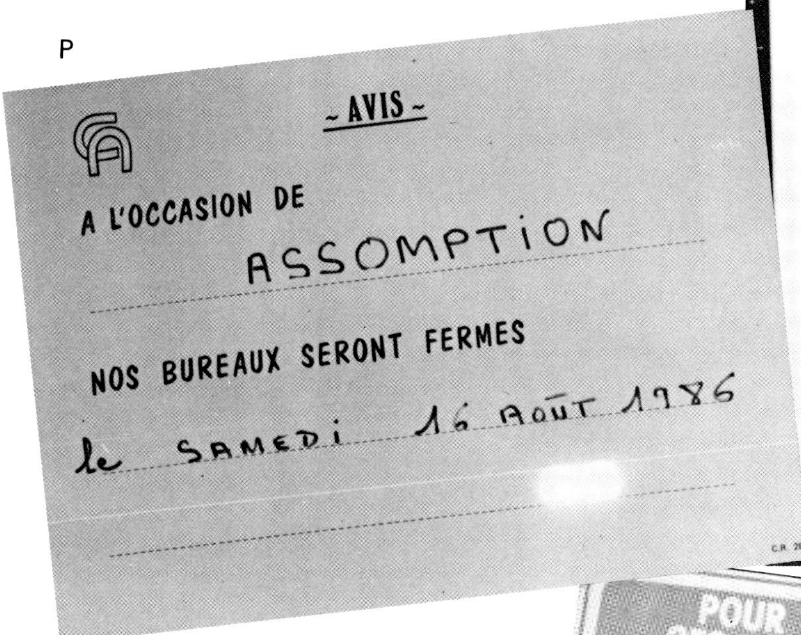

R

Q

S

At the market

1 What is being sold at stall **A**?
2 What two things are you told about the popcorn on sale in **B**?

3 During a camping holiday in France your Mum asks you to visit the market and buy some fresh food. In English, list four of the vegetables for sale on stall **C**.

4 You are on holiday in France and decide to buy something for your evening meal in market **D**.
   a How much would you pay for 5 kilograms of tomatoes?
   b What costs 2 francs for 2 kilograms?

5 You have 20 francs. Would it be possible to buy four melons at stall **E**?

6 What is being sold for 10 francs a kilogram in **F**:

   a garlic
   b green beans
   c potatoes
   d apples?

7 Walking through market **G** you feel like eating some peaches.

   a What is the lowest price for 1 kilogram?
   b What is the highest price for 1 kilogram?

8 When you arrive for a camping holiday in the South of France, you find you have forgotten your socks. What is the cheapest price you would pay for three pairs on market stall **H**?

E

G

F

H

9 You spot stall **I** in a market and decide to buy a jumper:
   a How much change would you receive from a 100 franc note?
   b What else is being sold, in addition to jumpers?

I

Labels

Look at the labels on these pages and answer the questions.

1 **a** What is commodity **A**?
  b Does it have any fragrance?
  c What will it do to your skin?
2 **a** Is **B** a mild shampoo?
  b How will it leave your hair?
3 What warning is given in **C**?
4 **a** What do you think **D** is?
  b What two instructions are given?

D

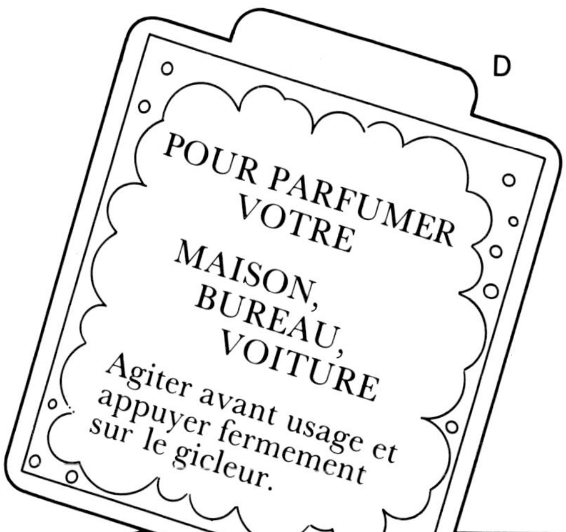

A

C

B

5 **a** What would you find in packet **E** in two colours?
b What are these colours?
c What is said about their thickness?

6 To which part of your body would you apply product **F**?

7 **a** What is in the bottle labelled **G**?
b How are you advised to store it?

8 **a** What is in the bottle labelled **H**?
b What are you told about its composition?

9 Would garment **I** be suitable for a child or for an adult?

10 How are you told to clean garment **J**?

11 What must you *not* do with the jumper labelled **K**?

12 According to label **L**:
a Should you soak this jumper?
b What must you do while it is still damp?

J

NE PAS NETTOYER
A SEC

E

500 MOUCHOIRS
en papiers couleurs
rose et rouge
(Double épaisseur)

F

UTILISER
REGULIEREMENT
SUR LES MAINS

H

VIN DE TABLE ROUGE
(25 cl).
Mélange de vins de différents
pays de la Communauté
Européenne.
Mis en bouteille par ASD.

G

BIERE BRUNE
25 cl.
Produite et embouteillée par
Neston, Menton, France
Mettez au réfrigérateur et buvez frais

K

Ne pas sécher
en machine.
Ne pas frotter ni tordre.
Rincer à l'eau froide.

I

Hauteur 112 cm
Tour de poitrine
56 cm

L

** NE PAS FAIRE*
TREMPER
** BIEN RINCER*
Remettre en forme
encore humide

Entertainment

Television and radio

1 Article **A** is from the French magazine *Marie-France*. Read it carefully and answer the questions:

a What does the caption mean in English?
b What has Great Britain received 26 times?
c Describe what is said about *Dallas* and *Dynasty*.
d What did the English do in 1985?
e Give two reasons for this success.
f State three facts about BBC1 and one fact about BBC2 mentioned in the article.
g How many commercial TV stations are mentioned and what is said about those in London.
h How long according to the article has Channel 4 been in operation?
i Summarise what is said in the third column, from 'financée par la publicité' to 'Et justement, ça tourne!'

A

GRANDE-BRETAGNE
La meilleure télévision du monde

C'est la référence ! Les Anglais ont la meilleure télévision du monde. Pourquoi ? Peut-on comparer ? Comment ? Pour la qualité des programmes il existe le prix Italia, récompense suprême, qui, depuis l'après-guerre, est revenu 26 fois à la Grande-Bretagne contre 9 fois à la France et la Suède ex-aequo. Ensuite, peuple chauvin, les téléspectateurs britanniques préfèrent leurs propres feuilletons comme « Le joyau de la couronne » (sur la fin de l'Empire des Indes) aux produits phares américains. En terme d'audience, « Dallas » et « Dynasty » n'arrivent chaque semaine qu'entre la 9e et la 25e place. Enfin, les Anglais exportent. Beaucoup. Depuis les années 80, les chiffres s'envolent ! En 85, ils ont fait 26 fois plus fort que les Français !
Pourquoi ce succès ? Cela tient à la créativité des cinéastes outre-Manche. Et à est chargée de fabriquer trois journaux par jour à destination du réseau puisque ces compagnies sont regroupées au sein de l'ITV, Indépendant Television. Pour chapeauter la chose, une autorité appelée IBA règle avec précision la vocation de chaque station, limite les rediffusions et exige chaque année, une certaine quantité et qualité de nouvelles émissions à produire.
Mieux. Depuis 3 ans, IBA a sa filiale, la quatrième chaîne de télévision Channel l'organisation de la télévision britannique. Les deux chaînes de service public, BBC 1 et BBC 2 sont complémentaires. BBC 1 est grand public, (35 % de l'audience). C'est elle qui a racheté « Dallas ». Elle qui crée une série maison « East Enders » fleuron de l'humour cockney. BBC 2 est plus culturelle (9-10 % d'audience).
A côté de cela, il existe dix-sept stations Four. Financée par la publicité du réseau ITV, Channel 4 est chargée de stimuler la création. Ainsi depuis quelques années, des centaines, voire des milliers de petites boîtes de production indépendantes naissent et vivent de la manne tombée des budgets ITV ou Channel 4. Recherche d'une assise populaire pour le service public, et obligation de création pour les télévisions commerciales... avouez que les Britanniques ont le sens du paradoxe. Et justement, ça tourne !
de télévision commerciale. Certaines sont riches et ont une large couverture géographique. D'autres sont spécialisées. Une station s'occupe des programmes du matin TV-AM. Deux se partagent Londres : l'une en semaine et l'autre le dimanche (London TV-Week-end). Une autre enfin

Sophie Viel

2 You are on holiday in France, and decide to listen to the radio. Picking up *Le Monde* you read article **B** which gives details about *France-Musique*.

a On which day does the station start latest?
b When do programmes continue after midnight?
c On Saturday what two sorts of music could you hear?
d What exactly could you listen to between 7.02 am and 9.10 am on Sunday?
e How many different composers are featured on Sunday?
f What precisely would you hear on *L'imprévu* at 7.10 am on Monday, Tuesday and Wednesday?
g Imagine your friend does not understand French. Could you explain what is on the air: at 8.30 am on Tuesday? at 3.30 pm on Wednesday?
h Music from several parts of the world is featured on Wednesday. Which countries are represented?

B

France-Musique

SAMEDI 19 AVRIL

2.00 Les nuits de France-Musique : Lettres et journaux intimes.
7.02 Avis de recherche :
9.10 Carnet de notes.
11.00 Œuvres de Leos Janacek.
12.05 Désaccord parfait : débat sur Bruckner ; à 14 h, concert : œuvres de Bruckner, Brahms, Wolf, Reger, par l'ensemble vocal Michel Piquemal.
15.00 Le temps du jazz : jazz s'il vous plaît ; Hexagonal, tendances de la saison 85-86 du jazz français.
16.00 Opéra : « Narcisso, amor d'un ombra e gelosia d'un aura » de Scarlatti, par la Grande Ecurie et Chambre du Roi, dir. J.-C. Malgoire.
19.05 Les cinglés du music-hall : Ultraphone ultra-chic.
20.04 Avant concert.
20.30 Concert (donné à la radio de Berlin le 10 mai 1985) : « Tic-toc-toc ou les Maillotins », « les Barricades mystérieuses » de Couperin, « le Coucou », de L.-C. d'Aquin, « la Poule », « le Rappel des oiseaux », « les Cyclopes », de Rameau, « Miroirs », de Ravel, « Vingt regards sur l'Enfant Jésus », extraits de Messiaen, « Etudes symphoniques en forme de variations », de Schumann, par Anne Queffélec au piano.
23.00 Les soirées de France-Musique : archives, Hermann Scherchen, chef d'orchestre ; à 1.00, Champs d'étoiles, voyage à travers la chanson

DIMANCHE 20 AVRIL

2.00 Les nuits de France-Musique : La Suisse.
7.02 Concert-promenade : musique viennoise et musique légère.
9.10 Musique sacrée : « Œuvres de J.-S. Bach.
10.00 Touche pas à mon héros : génie et métamorphoses de Franz Liszt, de la comète au baiser de Beethoven.
12.05 Magazine international.
14.05 Top laser : œuvres de Rameau, J.-S. Bach, Mozart, Haydn, Massenet, Bizet, Gounod...
17.00 Comment l'entendez-vous ? : 30 ans de carrière, œuvres de Donizetti, Massenet, Bizet, Gounod...
19.05 Jazz vivant.
20.04 Concert (donné salle Favart à Paris les 22 et 23 mars) : « L'écume des jours » d'Edison Denisov, par les Chœurs et l'orchestre de l'Opéra de Paris, dir. J. Burdekin, et les chorales d'enfants CNR de Rueil-Malmaison et A tre Voci.
23.00 Les soirées de France-Musique : ex-libris ; à 1 h, les Hollywoodiens : Alfred Newman.

LUNDI 21 AVRIL

2.00 Les nuits de France-Musique : Lettres de Bohème.
7.10 L'imprévu : magazine d'actualité musicale.
9.05 Le matin des musiciens : Yvonne Lefébure, ses maîtres et ses élèves, histoire d'une vie : « Jouez ma musique ».
12.10 Le temps du jazz : le jazz par ailleurs.
12.30 Concert : œuvres de Scarlatti, Schutz, Haendel, par l'Orchestre baroque et les chœurs de chambre de Stuttgart.
14.02 Repères contemporains.
15.00 Les chants de la Terre : magazine des musiques traditionnelles et populaires.
15.30 Les après-midi de France-Musique : l'Octuor de l'Opéra de Vienne, œuvres de Mozart ; à 17 h, Paysage romantique : les héros dans la tourmente, Manfred.
18.02 Avis aux amateurs.
19.10 Premières loges : Eugène Bigot et les artistes lyriques.
20.04 Jazz d'aujourd'hui : Vient de paraître.
20.30 Concert (Festival Janequin, de Châtellerault, le 5 sept.) : « Pavane », « Gaillarde », « Martin menait son troupeau » de Janequin, « Pass'e mezzo antico » et « Moderno Saltarello », de Mainerio, « Suite extraite de « Musicque de Joye », de Moderne, « Basse dance-la-Brosse », d'Attaignant, « Canzon degli Uccelli », de Dalla Casa, « Suite extraite de « Het derde musyck boexken » de Susato, « Deux pièces en concert », de Terzi, par the Parley of instruments, dir. P. Holman, M. Caudle.
22.00 Les soirées de France-Musique : cycle acousmatique ; à 23.05, Radio-France et l'Année de l'Inde ; à 0.30, Le musicien de minuit, musiques amoureuses.

MARDI 22 AVRIL

2.00 Les nuits de France-Musique : musique catalane.
7.10 L'imprévu : magazine d'actualité musicale.
9.05 Le matin des musiciens : voir lundi.
12.10 Le temps du jazz : le jazz ailleurs, Japon, Argentine, Brésil et retour sur la Belgique.
12.30 Concert (le 10 décembre à Caen) : œuvres de Schoenberg, Berio, Gulda par l'ensemble instrumental de Basse-Normandie, dir. D. Debart.
14.02 Repères contemporains.
14.30 Les enfants d'Orphée : les métiers du théâtre.
15.00 Côté jardin : magazine de l'opérette.
15.30 Les après-midi de France-Musique : œuvres de Mozart par l'Octuor de l'Opéra de Vienne ; à 17 h, Paysage romantique, le chant du destin, œuvres de Liszt, Brahms, Mahler, Schubert.

17 MARDIS POUR FRANCE-MUSIQUE

18.30 XXe siècle : images de la musique française, en direct de l'auditorium 106, œuvres de Saint-Saëns, Daniel-Lesur, Jolivet par le Quatuor Viotti.
20.10 Jazz d'aujourd'hui : lecture au laser.
20.30 Musique ensembles (en direct du Grand auditorium) : « la Création du monde », de Milhaud, « Architectures colorées », de Guezec, « la Confession impudique », de Cavanna, « De Stijl », de Andriessen, « Gestalt 17 », de Matsushita par l'ensemble de musique vivante, dir. D. Masson, sol. I. Jarsky, B. Fabre-Garrus, A. Seriese, P. Larson, P. Stades, L. Harting.
22.30 Maurice Ohana l'œuvre pour piano (en direct du Grand Auditorium) : œuvres de Ohana et Debussy par J.-C. Pennetier au piano.
0.00 Les soirées de France-Musique : œuvres de Mozart, Smetana, Britten, Fauré.

MERCREDI 23 AVRIL

6.00 Musique légère.
7.10 L'imprévu : magazine d'actualité musicale.
9.05 Le matin des musiciens : voir lundi.
12.10 Le temps du jazz : le jazz ailleurs, Japon, Argentine, Brésil et retour sur la Belgique.
12.30 Concert (donné au Festival de Ludwigsburg, le 1er septembre) : œuvres de Mozart, Dvorak, Beethoven par le Quatuor de Cleveland.
14.02 Jeunes solistes : œuvres de J.-S. Bach, Pergolèse, Mozart, Brahms, Wagner... par M. Franceschi, soprano et I. Mancini, piano.
15.00 Acousmathèque : les nouveaux mystères du son, hallucinations.
15.30 Les après-midi de France-Musique : l'Octuor de l'Opéra de Vienne « l'Opéra de Richard Strauss », œuvres de Strauss et Weber ; à 17 h, Paysage romantique, œuvres de Schubert, Liszt, Mahler, Schumann, Wagner, Chopin, Strauss.
19.12 Répertoire italien : œuvres de Cherubini, Petrassi.
19.30 Spirales : magazine de la musique contemporaine.
20.04 Jazz d'aujourd'hui : où jouent-ils ?
20.30 Concert (en direct du Théâtre des Champs-Elysées) : « Symphonie n° 7 en mi mineur » de Mahler, par l'Orchestre national de France, dir. V. Neumann.
23.05 Les soirées de France-Musique : jazz club, en direct du « Petit Opportun ».

JEUDI 24 AVRIL

2.00 Les nuits de France-Musique : nuit napolitaine.
7.10 L'imprévu, magazine d'actualité musicale.
9.05 L'oreille en colimaçon.
9.20 Le matin des musiciens : voir lundi.
12.10 Le temps du jazz : le jazz ailleurs, Japon, Argentine, Brésil, et retour sur la Belgique.
12.30 Concert (donné au Festival de Montreux-Vevey le 4 octobre) : œuvres de Bartok, Ravel, Schubert,

3 C appears in *Le Monde* newspaper. Look at the details carefully and answer the questions:

- **a** At 8.30 pm on TF1 there is a programme based on the work of which writer?
- **b** What could you see at 8.35 pm on A2?
- **c** In which country was the FR3 film made?
- **d** What would you expect to see at 10.45 pm on FR3?
- **e** How many films are showing on Canal Plus?
- **f** Which of the listed programmes have appeared on British television?
- **g** *France-Culture* has a programme at 12.10 am, what would you call it in English?
- **h** Name six composers whose music you could hear on *France-Musique*.

C

Mardi 22 avril

PREMIÈRE CHAINE : TF 1

20 h 30 Les grands écrans de TF1 : Un petit paradis.
De M. Wyn, d'après le roman de G.-J. Arnoud, avec Y. Folliot, R. Berry, F. Chaumette... (rediff.).
Un jeune couple croit avoir trouvé la maison de ses rêves pour une bouchée de pain, les précédents locataires étant morts d'un accident de la route. Mais très vite ce petit paradis va se transformer en enfer...

22 h 5 Série : De la sainteté.
Série de quatre émissions de José-Maria Berzosa.
La quatrième, la plus belle émission de cette série sur la sainteté. José-Maria Berzosa regarde avec un mélange d'étonnement, d'ironie parfois et de tendresse le train-train ordinaire d'une canonisation. Il a reconstitué le miracle. La dévotion populaire dans toute sa simplicité et sa pureté.

23 h 5 Journal.

23 h 20 C'est à lire.

DEUXIÈME CHAINE : A2

20 h 35 Cinéma : le Retour du grand blond.
Film français d'Y. Robert (1974). Avec P. Richard, M. Darc, J. Rochefort, J. Carmet, M. Duchaussoy.
Le violoniste hurluberlu qui avait été enrôlé malgré lui dans les services secrets français fait les frais de la rivalité de deux officiers. Malgré des astuces de vaudeville, cela ne vaut pas le premier « grand blond ».

22 h Mardi cinéma.
Pour ses jeux et pour commenter l'actualité cinématographique, Pierre Tchernia a invité : Brigitte Fossey, Richard Berry, Michel Blanc et Jacques Villeret.

23 h 15 Journal.

TROISIÈME CHAINE : FR3

20 h 35 Cinéma : l'Homme de la loi.
Film américain de M. Winner (1970). Avec B. Lancaster, R. Ryan, L.J. Cobb, S. North.
Un shérif intransigeant veut absolument – contre l'opinion d'une petite ville – punir sept hommes responsables d'un meurtre. Douloureuse histoire d'un justicier qui provoque un carnage au nom du devoir, la mise en scène a subi la mauvaise influence du western italien.

22 h 15 Journal.

22 h 45 Emissions régionales.
A chaque région son programme.

23 h 40 Prélude à la nuit.

FR3 PARIS-ILE-DE-FRANCE

17 h, La mer buissonnière ; **17 h 15,** Série : Dynastie ; **18 h,** Effraction ; **18 h 55,** Croqu'soleil ; **19 h 5,** Atout PIC ; **19 h 15,** Informations ; **19 h 35,** L'homme au képi noir.

CANAL PLUS

20 h 30, A nous les garçons, film de M. Lang ; **22 h 25, Ça n'arrive qu'à moi,** film de F. Perrin ; **23 h 55, les Nuits de Lucrèce Borgia,** film de S. Grieco ; **1 h 40,** Série : Mike Hammer.

LA « 5 »

20 h 30 Les Hommes d'argent.
Série américaine, avec K. Douglas et A. Baxter (et à 0 h 10).

22 h 30 Jonathan.
Magazine de l'aventure (et à 1 h 55).

23 h 15 Série : Knight Rider.

TV6

14 h, 6 Tonic (et à 20 h) ; **17 h, Système 6 ; 19 h, NRJ 6** (et à 23 heures).

FRANCE-CULTURE

20 h 30 Le journal du corps.
21 h 30 Diagonales, l'actualité de la chanson.
22 h 30 Nuits magnétiques : la nuit et le moment ; les prisons.
0 h 10 Du jour au lendemain.

FRANCE-MUSIQUE

20 h 30 Musique ensembles (en direct du Grand Auditorium) : *la Création du monde,* de Milhaud ; *Architectures colorées,* de Guezec ; *la Confession impudique,* de Cavanna ; *De Stijl,* de Andriessen ; *Gestalt 17,* de Matsushita, par l'Ensemble de musique vivante, dir. D. Masson, sol. I. Jarsky, B. Fabre-Garrus, A. Seriese, P. Larson, P. Stades, L. Harting.

22 h 30 Maurice Ohana l'œuvre pour piano (en direct du Grand Auditorium) : œuvres de Ohana et Debussy, par J.-C. Pennetier au piano.

0 h Les soirées de France-Musique : œuvres de Mozart, Smetana, Britten, Fauré.

The cinema

1 On holiday in the south of France you decide to see a film. **A** and **B** are advertisements in *Nice-Matin,* a newspaper popular in the area.

- **a** When is *Karate Kid* showing?
- **b** Translate the two rules which accompany this advertisement.
- **c** What happens at *UGC Variétés* on 9 August?
- **d** What does the sub-title for *Yiddish Connection* mean in English?
- **e** Translate the words under the picture and state when the last performance takes place.

A

B

2 What two pieces of important information are given on the cinema door in **C**?

C

3 **D** is a page from a French newspaper which gives information on a variety of films. Read it carefully and try to answer these questions:

- **a** What advantage would there be in going to *Calypso I* and *II* on a very hot day?
- **b** What time is the latest film showing in Carqueiranne?
- **c** Work out how many films, showing in Hyères, were made in English.
- **d** Why would you expect young children to enjoy the 2.30 pm performance at *Olbia 2*?
- **e** When is the earliest showing of a film in Saint-Raphaël, and when is the latest showing?
- **f** Which Toulon cinema has the largest number of films showing?
- **g** Looking at all the films showing, which would you say was: the most popular film? the next most popular film?

Cinémas

► *BORMES-LES-MIMOSAS*

CALYPSO 1 (la Favière, plein air). — Séance à 21.15 : **Karaté Kid II.**

CALYPSO 2 (la Favière, salle climatisée). — Séance à 21.15 : **Vampire vous avez dit vampire.** 23.30 : **Tenue de soirée.**

► *BRIGNOLES*

KAT 1 et 2. — Relâche.

LES 400 COUPS. — 17.00 : **Le bonheur a encore frappé.** 21.00 : **Amadeus.**

► *CARQUEIRANNE*

LE RIVIERA. — 21.00 : **Si t'as besoin de rien fais-moi signe.** 23.00 : **Vampire vous avez dit vampire.**

LE PLEIN AIR. — 21.30 : **Le Contrat.**

► *COGOLIN*

LES MARINES. — 21.30 : **Police Academy n° 3.** 23.30 : **Le Contrat.**

► *DRAGUIGNAN*

ELDO 1. — 21.30 : **Short Circuit.**

ELDO 2. — 21.30 : **D.A.R.Y.L.**

► *FRÉJUS*

VOX 1. — 16.00, 20.30 et 22.30 : **Karaté Kid II.**

VOX 2. — 16.00, 20.30 et 22.30 : **Short Circuit.**

VOX 3. — 16.00, 20.30 et 22.30 : **Police Academy n° 3.**

► *GASSIN*

CINÉMA DE VERDURE (R.N. 98, entrée de Saint-Tropez). — 21.30 : **Highlander.**

► *HYÈRES*

EDEN 1. — 20.00 et 22.15 : **Campus.**

EDEN 2. — 20.00 et 22.15 : **Le Diable au corps.**

EDEN 3. — 21.30 : **Out of Africa.**

FEMINA 1. — 15.00 et 21.30 : **Short Circuit.**

FEMINA 2. — 15.00 et 21.30 : **Drôles d'espions.**

FEMINA 3. — 15.00 et 21.30 : **Les anges sont pliés en dieux.**

OLBIA 1. — 14.30, 19.30 et 21.40 : **Karaté Kid II.**

OLBIA 2. — 14.40 et 19.30 : **Cendrillon.**

OLBIA 3. — 21.40 : **Police Academy 3.**

OLBIA 4. — 14.30, 19.30 et 21.40 : **L'Aigle de fer.**

LES ILES D'OR (la Capte). — 21.00 : **Short Circuit.**

► *LE LAVANDOU*

LEVENDOR (place de la Gare-des-Cars). — 21.15 : **Drôles d'espions.**

LES CYCLADES (en plein air). — 21.15 : **P.R.O.F.S.**

► *LA LONDE-LES-MAURES*

CINÉMA DE PLEIN AIR. — 21.15 : **Rocky IV.**

► *LE LUC*

LE CINÉMA. — Relâche.

► *LE PRADET*

CINÉMA EN PLEIN AIR. — 21.30 : **Youngblood.**

► *PORT-GRIMAUD*

LE STUDIO (place de l'Eglise). — 21.15 : **Trois Hommes et un couffin.** — 23.15 : **L'Exorciste.**

► *SAINTE-MAXIME*

LE MAXIME (rue P.-Curie). — 21.30 : **Short Circuit.**

► *SAINT-RAPHAËL*

CASINO. — 20.00 : **School Girls** ; 21.45 : **Terminator** ; 23.45 : film « X » (+ 18 ans).

RIALTO 1. — 15.00, 20.00, 22.20 : **Karaté Kid 2.**

RIALTO 2. — 15.00, 20.00, 22.10 : **Drôles d'espions.**

RIALTO 3. — 15.00, 20.00, 22.15 : **Le Diable au corps.**

LIDO 1. — 15.00, 20.00, 22.15 : **Short Circuit.**

LIDO 2. — 15.00, 20.00 : **Trois Hommes et un couffin.** 22.15 : **Si t'as besoin de rien, fais-moi signe.**

LIDO 3. — 15.00, 20.00, 22.15 : **Le Contrat.**

CINÉMA DE VERDURE (bd de la Plage, Agay). — 21.15 : **Les Mines du roi Salomon.**

► *SAINT-TROPEZ*

RENAISSANCE. — 21.15 : **Karaté Kid II.**

► *SALERNES*

LA TOMETTE. — Relâche.

► *TOULON*

ARIEL (tél. 94.93.52.22). — **Cléopâtre ; Karaté Kid 2 ; Si t'as besoin de rien, fais-moi signe ; Campus 86 ; Trois Hommes et un couffin ; Highlander.**

COMŒDIA (tél. 94.41.00.81). — **Soleil vert ; A double tranchant ; Contes immoraux ; Bananas ; The Blue Brothers.**

DRIVE-IN-CINÉ (La Farlède). — Relâche.

FEMINA (tél. 94.92.39.31). — **Karaté Kid 2 ; Police Academy n° 3 ; Out of Africa ; 37°2 le matin ; L'Aigle de fer ; St-Elmo's Fire ; Profession génie ; La Loi de Murphy ; Rambo I ; Deux Nuits de plaisir ; Horor Story.**

GAUMONT (tél. 94.92.21.88). — **Psychose ; Mona Lisa ; Le Contrat ; Cendrillon ; Drôles d'espions ; Hitcher.**

RAIMU (tél. 94.92.21.42). — **D.A.R.Y.L. ; Gung Ho ; Bons Baisers de Russie.**

REX. — Quatre films « X » (+ 18 ans).

ROYAL (tél. 94.91.06.98). — Trois films « X » (+ 18 ans).

UTOPIA (tél. 94.62.39.13). — SALLE 1 : **Le Diable au corps ; Opera do Malandro ; Prends l'oseille et tire-toi.** — SALLE 2 : **Prends l'oseille et tire-toi ; L'Ame sœur ; Voyage au bout de l'enfer.**

D

The theatre

During a stay in France you decide to go to a theatre. Look at advertisements **A–D**, and answer the questions:

1 **a** How would you translate the title of play **A**?
   b What is the opinion expressed by *Télérama*?
   c Who wrote the play?

2 **a** For how long is play **B** showing?
   b What do you understand by '50 Représentations Exceptionelles'?

3 **a** Name the author of **C**.
   b For how long is the play running and where is the theatre found?

4 **a** According to **D** when does *Poil de Carotte* commence and how many days a week is it showing?
   b What are the opinions of *Le Figaro, Le Parisien,* and *Télé 7 Jours* on the play?

A

C

B

D

5 The *Café d'Edgar* provides a good selection of entertainment. You are going out with some friends and they ask you to tell them what is showing. Read **E** and answer these questions:

- **a** For how long has the 8.15 pm performance been showing?
- **b** What does *France Soir* say about the 9.30 pm performance?
- **c** If you went to the 10.30 pm show, what would you expect to hear?

6 Look at advertisement **F** and decide whether these statements are true or false:

- **a** Ou peut voir le spectacle le 8 août.
- **b** *Bonjour de Tahiti* se montre pour quatre jours.

7 **G** is an advertisement for a concert.

- **a** When exactly could you see this concert?
- **b** For how long could you dance and how many musicians would there be?
- **c** Name two people in the *Archie Shepp Septet*.

E

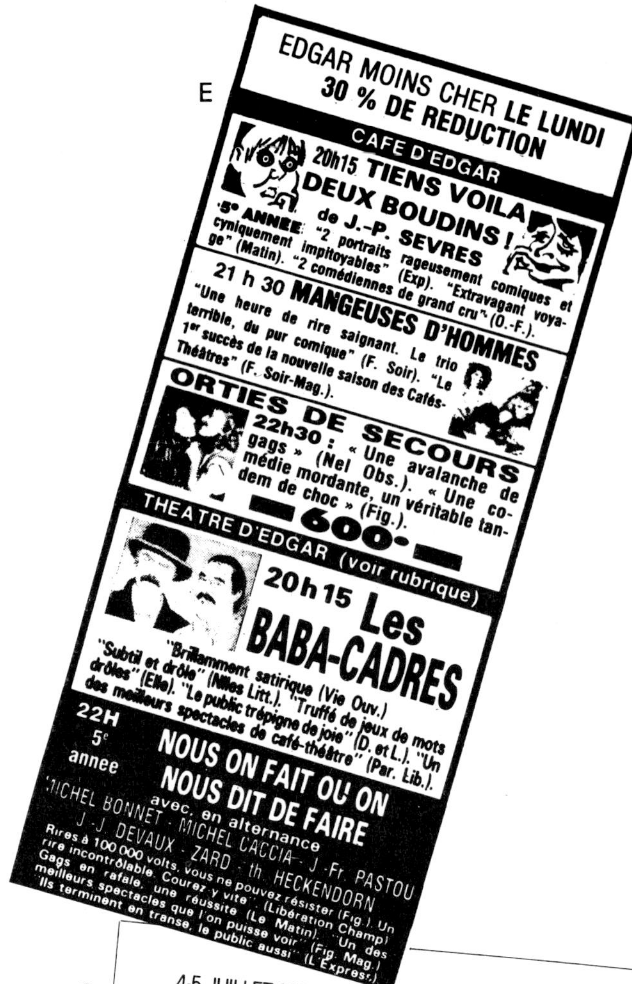

F

G

8 Advertisement **H** comes from *Le Monde*. Read it and answer the following questions:

- **a** Which English orchestra is mentioned?
- **b** Name two English composers whose music you could hear on 22 and 26 April.
- **c** What instrument does Claude Helffer play?
- **d** If you liked music by Haydn, on what day and at what time would you have to arrive at the concert hall?
- **e** When is Gwyneth Jones appearing in Paris?
- **f** Which instruments are played by Paul Meyer and Philippe Cassard?

H

CALENDRIER DES ADMINISTRATEURS DE CONCERTS

THÉATRE MUSICAL DE PARIS CHATELET Mardi 22 samedi 26 avril à 20 h 30 (p.e. Valmalète)	LONDON SINFONIETTA OPERA ORCHESTRA Dir. : ANTONY PAY Sol. : NEIL JENKINS ténor Le 22 : ROSSINI, ELGAR BRITTEN, TIPPETT Le 26 : ROSSINI, ELGAR VAUGHAM WILLIAMS, BRITTEN	ÉGLISE DES BILLETTES dimanche 27 avril à 17 heures (p.e. Kiesgen)	OPUS ENSEMBLE DONIZETTI – C. Ph. E. BACH HONEGGER
SALLE GAVEAU Jeudi 24 avril à 20 h 30 (p.e. Kiesgen)	J.-M. Fournier Productions Récital de piano Claude HELFFER RAMEAU - BRAHMS DEBUSSY - XENAKIS	THÉATRE MUSICAL DE PARIS CHATELET Lundi 28 avril à 20 h 30 (p.e. Valmalète) OPÉRA ET CONCERT	Gwyneth JONES Geoffrey PARSONS Piano BERG, DUPARC BRITTEN, STRAUSS
ÉGLISE DE LA MADELEINE Jeudi 24 avril à 21 heures (p.e. Valmalète)	CONCERTS LAMOUREUX HAYDN : LA CRÉATION Chorale E. BRASSEUR Sol. : A. CSENGERY N. TULLER M. HILL Dir. : Robert MARTIGNONI	THÉATRE DU MUSÉE GRÉVIN Lundi 28 avril à 20 h 30 Loc. tél. : 42-46-84-47 3 FNAC (p.e. Valmalète)	3 concerts par DEVY ERLIH 1er concert : STRAVINSKI, WEBERN BERG, BARTOK PAUL MEYER clarinette PHILIPPE CASSARD piano

Sport

1 What is the French name for the game in **A**?
2 What is this Sunday newspaper advertising in **B**?

A

B

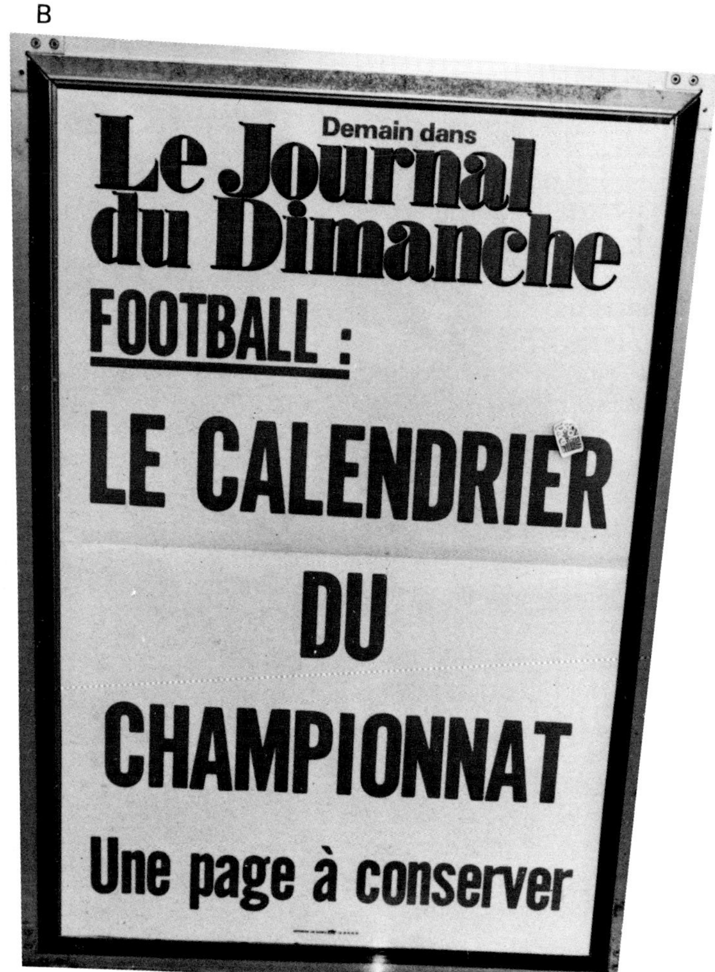

L'O.G.C. Nice à Nantes

"Faire un résultat"

Depuis hier soir les Niçois sont à Nantes. Ils séjournent à l'hôtel P.L.M. Carquefoux, après avoir pris un avion à 17 h 10 à l'aéroport de Nice.

Dans la matinée, Sérafin avait réuni ses treize joueurs pour un entraînement basé sur la vitesse. Ce matin, à 10 heures, dans un espace vert près de l'hôtel, il leur fera suivre un travail de tonification. Un quart d'heure pour stimuler les organismes.

Tout en les ménageant.

Le mot d'ordre lancé à travers l'Hexagone est: récupération. Avec ces matches qui se suivent à un rythme infernal, il importe de récupérer le plus vite possible. Sérafin pense que seuls passeront ceux qui auront un effectif suffisant pour 'tourner' ceux qui sauront garder leurs forces intactes.

Récupérer est une affaire de repos, évidemment. Mais aussi de nourriture. Savoir manger n'est pas à la portée de n'importe qui.

Et si les joueurs se sont réunis, vendredi après le match pour dîner ensemble, c'était surtout pour qu'ils aient un menu approprié: potage, saint-pierre grillé, salade de fruits.

Pour l'heure, ça ne va pas trop mal. Les organismes semblent avoir bien assimilé les deux premières rencontres.

C'est une bonne chose: ce soir, il faudra disposer de tous ses atouts face à un Nantes qui s'annonce redoutable.

Redoutable. C'est le mot utilisé par Michel Joly, qui est allé superviser les Nantais, vendredi dernier, à Toulon. Il a été impressionné par l'équilibre de l'équipe, par l'organisation offensive, avec Anziani et Garande opérant dans une position excentrée, mais il a été surtout impressionné par Olarticoechea et Burruchaga.

Un Burruchaga qui est sur la lancée du Mundial et qui a survolé le match.

Les Niçois savent donc ce qui les attend. Ils espèrent pourtant 'faire un bon résultat'.

L'équipe sera la suivante: Amitrano, Rico, Dreossi, Curbelo, Blanc, Oleksiak, Massa, Bernad, Henry, Cabrera et Pascal. 12: Mège. 13: Moralès.

Nantes: Bertrand-Demanes, Kombouaré, Le Roux, Der Zakarian, Olarticoechea, Debotté, Bracigliano, Burruchaga, Morice, Garande et Anziani. 12: Frankowski; 13: Robert. J.G.

'Nice-Matin'.

3 You meet a supporter of Nice football team in a French café and begin to discuss the game. He shows you newspaper **C**. See how much you understand.

- **a** Where are the Nice players staying in Nantes?
- **b** What happened at 10 o'clock, and where did it take place?
- **c** In paragraph three what reason is given for players recuperating as quickly as possible?
- **d** On which two things does recuperation depend?
- **e** What is considered to be appropriate food for players?
- **f** Which players impressed Michel Joly the most?
- **g** What do Nice hope for?

4 Poster **D** is advertising a lottery.

- **a** How many lotteries *Sportif* have already been held?
- **b** Where will the next draw be broadcast?

D

5 You are on holiday with your parents and come across notice **E**. Explain it to your Mum and Dad:

a Where and when does the event take place?

b Who is organising it and which star will appear?

c How much will they have to pay and how much will it cost for the car?

E

Pop music

A

1 Give the date and time of rock show **A**.

2 While on a four-day holiday in France you and your friends decide to go to a disco.
Notices **B–D** give details of the local discos.

- **a** Could you attend **B** on Mondays? For how many hours is it open?
- **b** Could you go to **C** every night? What time does it open?
- **c** On which days is disco **D** closed? What are its hours of opening? What happens on Sundays? What sort of dress is expected?

B

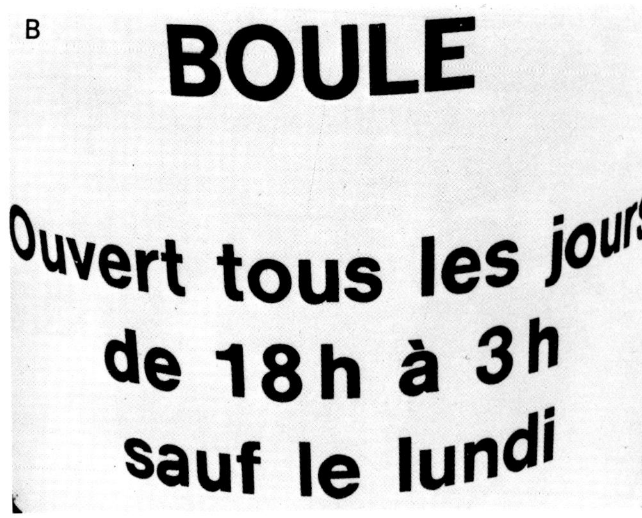

C

D

3 Read extracts **E** and **F** on Samantha Fox and Rod Stewart. Your friend asks you to explain since he cannot understand French. Summarise in English what is said in each article.

SAMANTHA FOX

Cette demoiselle très sexy nous vient d'Angleterre. Les radios FM nous diffusent son tube à longueur de temps. "Touch Me", son premier disque, est fait pour danser, pour bouger; très bien réalisé, c'est un excellent produit anglo-saxon.

Sam est née le 15 avril 1966, à Londres, où très jeune, elle se fait remarquer par son regard félin sans compter son physique de rêve. Ainsi elle connaît très tôt les studios où elle pose et devient top modèle. Mais elle veut aller plus loin et se lance dans le show-business.

Son album, qui est connu à peu près partout, est un succès. Accompagné d'un clip-vidéo, ce disque dévoile toutes les faces cachées de la belle Samantha.

ROD STEWART

De retour sur scène, Rod Stewart se prépare pour une super tournée de concerts en France. Nous l'avons rencontré pour vous. Pour le moment, il profite de ses vacances à Hollywood où il se repose. Car depuis 1969, il faut le signaler, sa moyenne est d'au moins un disque par an.

Il a toujours été fier de ses racines écossaises, bien que né dans la capitale anglaise. D'origine modeste, il se destinait au football mais le destin en voulut autrement. Après avoir été interprète de Jeff Beck Group, il créa le groupe Faces avec Ron Wood et Ronnie Lane, puis vola de ses propres ailes vers le succès et les disques d'or. Son dernier album est principalement consacré à la guitare et à son inimitable voix rauque. Censuré par les radios anglaises un certain temps à cause de ses paroles un peu osées, ce disque est devenu un succès total.

A 40 ans, toujours accompagné de jolies femmes, il nous fait profiter de sa joie de vivre, de son énergie et de ses super concerts.

School

Signs and timetables

1 Notice **A** appears outside a French school. Give the age range of the children you would find there.

2 Timetable **B** comes from a CES school:

- **a** How many foreign language lessons are there a week?
- **b** How much time is devoted to practical subjects?
- **c** This timetable differs from those found in British schools. State three *main* differences.

A

B

HEURE	LUNDI	MARDI	MERCREDI	JEUDI	VENDREDI	SAMEDI
de 8h à 9h	Français		Travaux manuels	Mathématiques	Allemand	Musique
de 9h à 10h	Français	Géographie	Travaux manuels	Histoire	Physique	Histoire
de 10h à 11h	Dessin	Anglais		Géographie	Physique	Géographie
de 11h à 12h	Mathématiques	Musique			Education physique	
de 13.50 à 14.50	Anglais	Biologie		Français	Permanence	
de 14.50 à 15.50	Gymnastique	Biologie		Dessin		
de 15.50 à 16.50		Histoire		Allemand	Mathématiques	

3 **C** is a typical Lycée timetable for a person in Classe de Terminale:

a Il a combien d'heures de sport par semaine?

b Il finit à quelle heure le mercredi?

c On déjeune à quelle heure?

C

CLASSE DE TERMINALE

	LUNDI	MARDI	MERCREDI	JEUDI	VENDREDI
8H	MATHÉMATIQUES		PHILOSOPHIE	GÉOGRAPHIE	PHILOSOPHIE
9H	PHILOSOPHIE	MATHÉMATIQUES	ANGLAIS		PHILOSOPHIE
10H	PHILOSOPHIE	PHILOSOPHIE	MATHÉMATIQUES	ESPAGNOL	HISTOIRE
11H	GÉOGRAPHIE	HISTOIRE	MATHÉMATIQUES	PHILOSOPHIE	SPORT
12H					
13H 30	ESPAGNOL			PHILOSOPHIE	MATHÉMATIQUES
14H 30		ANGLAIS		MATHÉMATIQUES	
15H	SPORT	ESPAGNOL		ANGLAIS	
16H	SPORT				

Rules and regulations

1 You are on a two-month exchange with a French person. On arrival at school you are given these rules in **A**. Read them carefully and try to answer these questions:

a What must pupils not do in corridors?
b Can you explain rule number 2?
c What are you told about punctuality?
d What is the procedure at the start of lessons?
e What sort of dress is required?
f What are pupils instructed to do with their homework?
g According to rule 7 what happens to pupils who do not work hard?
h What do you understand by rules 8 and 9?
i If you have time off school, what is the procedure you must follow?
j What is required of pupils in rule 11 and what could a teacher do to those who disregard the rules?
k Explain rule 12.

REGLEMENT INTERIEUR

1. Il est interdit de courir dans les couloirs.

2. Les élèves devront se montrer respectueux du règlement intérieur et de leurs professeurs.

3. Il faut arriver a l'heure en classe. Les élèves devront respecter les règles élémentaires de courtoisie et de ponctualité. Ils devront notamment se tenir en rang devant leurs salles 5 minutes avant la sonnerie marquant le début du cours.

4. Les élèves sont tenus de se présenter en cours dans une tenue vestimentaire décente.

5. Les élèves devront se tenir en rang devant les portes du réfectoire 10 minutes avant le premier service. Ils devront observer le plus grand silence possible afin de ne pas gêner leurs camarades dans les salles voisines.

6. Les élèves devront rendre en temps et en heures les devoirs donnés par leurs professeurs.

7. Si, au moment du conseil de classe de fin d'année, un professeur au moins, s'oppose au passage d'un élève en classe supérieure, celui-ci devra redoubler son année.

8. Expulsion temporaire—l'élève sera expulsé pendant une semaine, pour raison disciplinaire, à la demande du professeur concerné, après examen du cas par le conseil disciplinaire.

9. Il est interdit de fumer à l'intérieur des limites de l'établissement et de marcher sur les pelouses.

10. Toute absence doit être justifiée par un mot, des parents (ou tuteurs), ou du médecin en cas de maladie.

11. Les élèves doivent apporter une tenue de sport pour suivre dans dc bonnes conditions les Courts d'Education Physique et Sportive. Un élève pourrait se voir envoyé à l'étude par le professeur, si celui-ci juge sa tenue inadéquate à la pratique de l'éducation physique.

12. Le carnet de notes doit être tenu à jour par l'élève lui-même, qui chaque fin de mois doit le faire signer par ses parents.

A

Reports

1 A is André Chabry's school report, with comments made by the head teacher:

- **a** Which do you think is André's best subject?
- **b** Translate the comments made by the Geography and French teachers.
- **c** How could André improve his German?
- **d** Why is the PE teacher concerned about André?
- **e** What piece of advice is given by the Chemistry teacher?
- **f** What exactly does the Headmaster say?

A

LYCÉE FERNAND MALLET

Nom: CHABRY Prénom: ANDRÉ Classe: 3 II Année scolaire: 88/89

Effectif: 25

TROISIÈME TRIMESTRE

MATIÈRES	Conduite	Travail	Résultats Groupe	0 à 20	Appréciations
Maths	C	D	C	8	Il ne manifeste pas beaucoup d'intérêt pour l'algèbre
Chimie	B	C	C	7	Il faut faire plus d'effort. Il doit persévérer.
Géographie	D	C	C	8	Faible dans cette matière. Il doit étudier plus régulièrement. Élève trop bavard.
Histoire	B	B	B	14	Élève appliqué. Très bons résultats.
Français	B	C	C	11	Il doit lire plus en français. Il a des problèmes de compréhension
Allemand	B	C	B	10	Il a des problèmes avec les rédactions. Il doit étudier la grammaire.
Éducation physique	B	D			Il doit prendre cette matière plus au sérieux.

Observations de Monsieur le Directeur

Ensemble satisfaisant. Cependant des progrès devront être faits en Maths et en Chimie pour effectuer une bonne seconde.

2 Look at **B**. It shows that Marcel Picard has worked quite well in some subjects but has done little in others:

a What is Marcel like at spoken English?
b What encouragement is he given in French and Science by his teachers?
c Put into English what was written by the Music teacher and the Art teacher.
d What are the Headmaster's comments?

B

LYCÉE FERNAND MALLET

Nom. Picard... Prenom.. Marcel.. Classe. 3 I.. Année scolaire. 1988/89

Effectif.... 31......

TROISIÈME TRIMESTRE

MATIÈRES	Conduite	Travail	Résultats Groupe 0 à 20		Appréciations
Anglais	A	B	B	15	Fort à oral. Il est plutôt timide quand il parle en anglais
Français	A	A	A	17	Très bon résultats. Poursuivez l'effort
Travaux manuels	C	C	B	10	Résultats moyens. Élève dissipé
Musique	B	A	C	14	Il se débrouille bien au tambour. Il doit étudier le solfège
Maths	B	C	B	9	Il est très faible. Il a de grandes lacunes
Dessin	D	D	D	8	Peut mieux faire — élève turbulent
Sciences naturelles	A	B	C	14	Résultats dans l'ensemble assez satisfaisants — c'est un élève intéressé

Observations de Monsieur le Directeur

Cet élève a bien travaillé pendant tout le trimestre. Toutefois il faut qu'il fasse plus d'efforts en Mathématiques et en Dessin

Letters and events

1 While staying with a penfriend in Boulogne you attend an open day at her brother's school. **A** is the account of this in *La Semaine Boulonnais*. Read the newspaper article and try to answer these questions:

a When did the event occur and what sort of crowd attended?
b What did the pupils do?
c What jobs do these people have:
M. Pierre Pollet
M. Legrand
M. Fauquet?

MARQUISE

Gai, gai, l'écolier ; voilà les vacances !

A

Dimanche après-midi, au Groupe scolaire Pierre Mendes-France II, s'est déroulée la traditionnelle fête des prix des écoles publiques. Malgré quelques gouttes de pluie, une importante foule avait pris place autour du podium dressé dans la cour de l'établissement, afin de suivre le charmant spectacle de ballets, présenté par les enfants.
Parmi l'assistance, on pouvait notamment remarquer M. Pierre Pollet, maire de la commune, et ses adjoints et conseillers ; M. Carpentier, vice-président du conseil général et maire de Réty ; l'adjudant chef Luchez et le M.D.L. chef Legrand, de la brigade de gendarmerie locale ; M. Fauquet secrétaire général de la Mairie ; etc... A noter que la Lyre Marquisienne assura, avec talent, la partie musicale de cette après-midi particulièrement réussie.

B

Madame L Saumon
3, rue Marengo
54000 Nancy

Nancy, le 6 avril

Madame la Directrice
C.E.S. Henri Gardenal
Nancy

Madame la Directrice
Veuillez excuser l'absence de ma fille, Claudette, qui avait la grippe. Je lui fait garder le lit aussi pourra-t-elle retourner au collège d'ici une semaine.
Veuillez recevoir, Madame la Directrice, l'expression de mes sentiments respectueux,

L. Saumon

(Madame Saumon)

2 Claudette Saumon has been off school and her mother sends note **B**. What does the note tell the headmistress?

3 In **C** the Headmaster writes to Paul Langer's parents about a serious matter. Read the letter carefully:

- **a** What is the main complaint in the first sentence?
- **b** How does Paul react to homework?
- **c** In what way does he disturb classes?
- **d** What is his attitude towards staff?
- **e** What happened last week?
- **f** What does the Head teacher suggest and who should Monsieur and Madame Langer contact in the first instance?
- **g** Write a reply from Monsieur and Madame Langer, referring to the principal points raised by the Head teacher.

C

Saint-Omer le 20 avril

C. E. S. Dagneux
8, rue Montcalm,
62500 Saint-Omer

Monsieur et Madame Langer,
9, rue du Guide,
62500 Saint-Omer

Chers Monsieur et Madame,

Il ressort du dernier relevé de notes de votre fils Paul, que celui-ci ne se donne pas assez à son travail scolaire, à l'école de même qu'à la maison. Au dire de ses professeurs, Paul ne fait pratiquement jamais ses devoirs. De plus il arrive très souvent en retard, ce qui est une gêne considérable pour ses professeurs comme pour ses camarades, dont il interrompt les cours.

Et ceci n'est qu'un aspect de son évident manque de respect envers le personnel du collège. Par ailleurs, j'ai le regret de vous informer que Paul a fait l'école buissonière durant deux jours la semaine dernière.

Je pense qu'il est grand temps pour nous de nous rencontrer, dans l'intérêt de tous, et surtout dans l'intérêt de votre fils Paul. Je vous serais extrêmement reconnaissant de bien vouloir prendre contact avec mon secrétariat afin de convenir d'une entrevue au plus tôt.

En vous remerciant à l'avance de votre diligence et de votre comprehension, je vous prie d'agréer, Monsieur et Madame, l'expression de mes sentiments les meilleurs.

Marcel Monclar

Marcel Monclar
Proviseur

Holidays

Advertisements

1 **A** appears in a holiday brochure.
- **a** Name three creatures found in the district.
- **b** What two other attractions are there?

2 Look at advertisement **B**.
- **a** If you went on this holiday, how many days would you be away?
- **b** What are you told about January prices?
- **c** Which famous forest would you visit on this holiday?
- **d** Name two things you would find in a cabin.
- **e** Are any 'extra' trips included?
- **f** How would you book for this holiday?

B

A

3 Advertisement **C** comes from *Le Monde*.
- **a** What is the English name for 'Les Iles Anglo-Normandes'?
- **b** When is the best time to visit this area?
- **c** How many people live on the island described?
- **d** What are we told about St Helier?
- **e** Name three things tourists would find interesting in this town.

C

Mer

Iles Anglo-Normandes

ILE DE JERSEY

Le printemps est la période idéale pour profiter pleinement de cette adorable petite île (20 km sur 10 km, 76 000 habitants).

Les petits ports de pêche succèdent aux immenses plages de sable fin. La campagne est ravissante et fleurie. Dans la capitale, Saint-Hélier, un Londres en miniature, le shopping est roi. Les distractions sont innombrables, les auberges, les pubs sont pittoresques et les petites pensions voisinent avec les palaces de très grande classe.

Les Jersiais, cette année, vont concourir pour avoir le plus beau jardin, le plus beau parc, les villages, les écoles, les rues, les hôtels, les pubs... les mieux fleuris. Quel décor !

Et, toujours, le dépaysement, la détente et une qualité de vie particulière. Jersey vous attend : l'Ile Fleur ne demande qu'à être admirée et cueillie.

Pour documentation en couleur, écrivez à :
MAISON DE L'ILE DE JERSEY
Département F 6
19, boulevard Malesherbes, 75008 PARIS
TéL 47-42-93-68

4 You and your family decide to visit Provence. You find advertisement **D** in a newspaper.

- **a** What two facilities are on offer at *Mas de Garrigon*?
- **b** What would two weeks at the *Hôtels du Parc et du Centre* cost in spring?
- **c** What would be the cost in summer?

D

Provence

ROUSSILLON - 84220 GORDES

Le petit hôtel de charme du Luberon aux portes de la Haute-Provence et sa table gourmande.
Promenades. Piscine. Équitation. Tennis à 3 km. Séjour et week-end.
MAS DE GARRIGON ★★★
Tél. : 90-75-63-22
Accueil Christiane RECH.

30430 BARJAC

Le soleil à moins de 4 h par le TGV
HOTELS DU PARC ET DU CENTRE
Tél. 66-24-50-74 et 66-24-55-88.
Entièrement rénovés. Transfert AVIGNON-BARJAC gratuit. FORFAIT PRINTEMPS-AUTOMNE 14 jours de 1900 à 2000F net, pension complète, cinq excursions gratuites, animation quotidienne.
En JUILLET-AOUT : pension complète de 140 à 150F net avec une excursion par semaine, animation quotidienne, vin compris, piscine.
FORFAIT SUPER PROMOTION AUTOMNE de 13 jours à 2000F à partir du 9 octobre 1986 avec transport en autocar PARIS-BARJAC aller/retour.
Doc. P. BERTRAND, BP2, 30430 BARJAC.
Préciser la période choisie.

5 **E** comes from the 'Tourism' column in *Le Monde*.

- **a** In what part of France is Port-La-Nouvelle?
- **b** In the second advertisement, a young lady is asking for someone to share a holiday.
  Where is she going?
  How long will the holiday last?
  What would the holiday cost?
  How could you contact her?
- **c** What can you do at night at *Le Roumingue*?
- **d** What three sports are available at *Le Roumingue* and when would be the cheapest time to go there?

E

TOURISME

11210 PORT-LA-NOUVELLE
Magnifique plage sable fin du Midi. Ses meublés, ses hôtels, ses résidences
S.I.O.T. - B.P. 20
Tél. 68-48-00-51.

Jne femme 32 ans ch. coéquipier (ère) pour périple quatre semaines en Suède et Norvège, en voit., du 10 août au 4 sept. Coût du voyage : env. 12000 F par pers. Sér. référ. exig.
Ecr. sous réf. 10232 *le Monde* Publicité, 5, rue de Monttessuy, 75007 PARIS.

COTE ATLANTIQUE
BAIE D'ARCACHON
VILLAGE VACANCES grand confort CAMPING-CARAVANING
LE ROUMINGUE - 33138 LANTON
Tél. 56-82-97-48
Pension complète et demi-pension (vin compris) - Self-service - Buffet
DÉTENTE - REPOS - ANIMATION
Distractions variées adultes et enfants.
Plage priv. et surv. - Mini-golf - Tennis
Initiation planche à voile - Excursions
Soirées dansantes - Ciné - T.V. - Pêche.
Réductions en juin et septembre.

Planning a trip

1 You are staying with a French penfriend in Strasbourg and decide to take a holiday on the river Rhine. You discuss the contents of various brochures, and eventually decide on the trip advertised in **A**—a three-day trip from Strasbourg to Amsterdam on a KD company boat.

a Look at the plan of the vessel and translate the names of the different areas into English.
b According to the itinerary, what happens on day one of the trip?
c What do the details for day two tell you about: *la Pfalz*; Coblence; Bonn and Cologne?
d What information is given about Duisburg, Nimuège and Amsterdam?

A

KD German Rhine Line

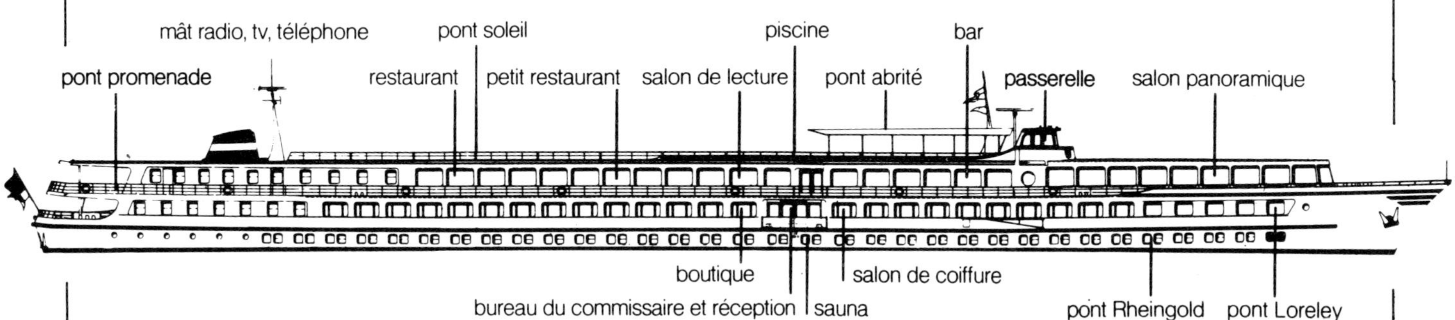

De Strasbourg à Amsterdam

Embarquement à Strasbourg, Gare Fluviale, de 19h30 à 22h00:

Mai	2	9	16	23	30
Juin	6	13	20	27	
Juillet	4	11	18	25	
Août	1	8	15	22	29
Septembre	5	12	19	26	
Octobre	3	10			

Dîner à bord. Début du voyage le lendemain matin.

1er jour: Strasbourg/3h15 – Rüdesheim/vers 15h45
Le bateau appareille très tôt le matin et, à l'heure du petit déjeuner, nous sommes déjà à Spire. De là, vous pouvez, si vous le désirez, participer à une excursion en autocar jusqu'à Heidelberg, ville universitaire fière de ses traditions. L'après-midi, le bateau longe les coteaux de vignobles du Palatinat et du Rheingau, ainsi que les villes de Mayence et de Wiesbaden. Une réception de bienvenue, donnée par le capitaine, figure également au programme. Après l' arrivée à Rüdesheim, vous aurez l'occasion de passer à terre quelques heures très agréables. Soirée dansante à bord.
* Excursion à Heidelberg; dép. de Spire 8h45 – arr. à Gernsheim 12h15; env. 29,50 DM
* Rüdesheim: visite de vignobles avec le »Winzer-Express« et visite du Salon musical mécanique de Siegfried: 15h45 env. 14,00 DM

2ème jour: Rüdesheim/8h30 – Cologne/vers 15h30
Cologne/17h45 – Düsseldorf/vers 20h15
Le matin, le bateau traverse l'étroit passage dans le massif schisteux rhénan. Vous voyez des petits villages viticoles pleins de charme, des vignobles, des châteaux moyenâgeux, la Pfalz, forteresse douanière au milieu du Rhin, et le rocher de la Lorelei. Plus tard, nous passons devant Coblence, à l'embouchure de la Moselle, et puis devant le Siebengebirge et Bonn, la capitale fédérale. Vous pourrez visiter Cologne, avec sa cathédrale, dans l'après-midi, et l'élégante ville de Düsseldorf le soir.
* Visite de Cologne en autocar; 15h30; env. 19,50 DM
* Visite de Düsseldorf en autocar; 21h00; env. 16,50 DM

3ème jour: Düsseldorf/3h15 – Amsterdam/vers 16h00
La silhouette imposante des gigantesques installations industrielles de la Ruhr, puis, Duisburg, le plus grand port intérieur du monde, constituent le décor de ces premières heures du jour. Peu de temps après, nous atteignons la frontière hollandaise, et dépassons Nimègue alors que le bateau glisse dans un paysage typiquement hollandais avec des moulins à vent, des digues et des canaux. En naviguant sur le canal qui relie le Rhin à Amsterdam, nous approchons du but de notre voyage: Amsterdam, ville très attrayante avec ses «Grachten», qui constituera l'un des grands moments de ce périple sur le Rhin, si riche en impressions.

2 You are on a school trip to the Champagne area of France and your teacher has obtained some information on the region **B**, and map **C**. Study it carefully and answer these questions:

- **a** How many départements are there in Champagne-Ardenne?
- **b** How many people live in the district and what area does it cover?
- **c** Name three tourist attractions in Les Ardennes.
- **d** Give the name of one type of food popular in the Ardennes.
- **e** Whereabouts is Troyes situated in the Aube district?
- **f** How many churches and museums would you find in Troyes?
- **g** What is grown on the plain of Marne?
- **h** Name the administrative centre of Marne.
- **i** Give two reasons why Reims is famous?
- **j** For what is Le Bassigny renowned?
- **k** What would you expect to find in Bourbonne-les-Bains?

B

CHAMPAGNE-ARDENNE *le pays où pétille la vie*

La CHAMPAGNE ARDENNE éveille tout d'abord dans l'esprit de chacun les bulles dorées d'un vin pétillant et léger, le champagne, vin des Rois et roi des vins. Viennent ensuite les images de forêts immenses et profondes se reflétant dans les eaux brillantes et limpides des nombreux lacs et cours d'eau qui coulent parmi les schistes et les calcaires. Ces calcaires dans lesquels ont été creusées des milliers de kilomètres de galeries où s'élabore et se bonifie le Vin de Champagne, et qui donnent les molles ondulations de la plaine champenoise.

La Champagne-Ardenne est organisée en 4 départements : Ardennes, Aube, Marne et Haute-Marne. La préfecture de la Région se trouve à Châlons-sur-Marne.

La superficie de la Champagne-Ardenne est de 25 600 km2 avec une population de 1 346 000 habitants.

La Région s'étire en latitude (100 à 170 km de large sur 330 km environ de long) de la Belgique aux portes de la Bourgogne.

Chaque département possède une carte d'identité propre, très originale. Pour le touriste, ils se complètent harmonieusement comme les pièces d'un puzzle pour former un tableau varié et enrichissant.

Les ARDENNES

Une superficie de 5 230 km2 pour 300 000 habitants.

Les Ardennes jouent la carte du Tourisme, ce qui va donner un essor nouveau à son économie. Le menu est copieux : de profondes forêts, refuges d'un abondant gibier, la Meuse qui serpente, langoureuse, bordée par les hautes falaises du Massif schisteux, des lacs aux plages de sable fin pour les pêcheurs et les amateurs de sports à voile.
Le département des Ardennes, c'est aussi Sedan, Rocroi, les vieilles forteresses, Charleville-Mézières, Monthermé... le jambon des Ardennes, la tarte au sucre, la salade au lard, le boudin blanc, toute une gastronomie robuste.

L'AUBE

Une superficie de 6 000 km2 et une population de 290 000 habitants.

L'Aube, c'est le pays du Lac et du Parc Naturel Régional de la Forêt d'Orient, avec ses paysages nonchalants, ses rivières, ses autres forêts et sous-bois, ses châteaux (La Motte Tilly), son vignoble et son champagne aussi... TROYES se dresse en son centre, fière de ses richesses superbement mises en valeur, ses églises (9 au total, se visitent), ses Musées (Musée d'Art Moderne, de la Bonneterie, des Beaux-Arts, Pharmacie-Musée, Maison de l'Outil...), le secteur piétonnier où ruelles et maisons à pans de bois ont été sauvegardées et restaurées : un coeur magnifique !

La MARNE

Une superficie de 8 200 km2 et 544 000 habitants.

C'est le Pays du Champagne, aux mille visages : parcouru en son centre par la vaste plaine crayeuse couverte de champs de céréales, il est bordé à l'ouest par les Côtes du vignoble prestigieux, de forêts et de prairies tachetées de nombreux étangs et à l'est par le Perthois et l'Argonne. Le

Perthois voit ses lettres de noblesse redorées grâce à la réalisation du Lac du Der-Chantecoq de 4 800 Ha, vaste complexe sportif et touristique et qui sert d'écrin aux remarquables maisons et édifices à pans de bois tels que le Village-Musée de Ste-Marie-du-Lac.
Châlons-sur-Marne, cité administrative s'enorgueillit de posséder le magnifique Cloître de Notre-Dame-en-Vaux et Reims se dispute avec Epernay le titre de capitale du Champagne. Reims, ville des sacres, parmi les flèches et les tours lancées vers le ciel, est fière d'une cathédrale bénie qui lui apporte, cependant, celui envié de "Ville des Sacres".

La HAUTE-MARNE

Une superficie de 6 210 km2 et 210 700 habitants.

C'est le Département du Tourisme Vert, du retour à la Nature, le château d'eau de la Région. Il partage avec le Département de la Marne, le Lac du Der-Chantecoq.
Pâturages verdoyants, vastes plateaux couverts de cultures et de forêts, cloisonnés de vigoureuses lignes de côtes et de vallées aux fraîches rivières se succèdent au hasard des promenades.
Le Bassigny est un riche terrain de fouilles archéologiques ; Bourbonne-les-Bains, unique et vivante station thermale de la Région, Langres dans ses remparts renferme une cité à l'architecture Renaissance qui vit naître Diderot.

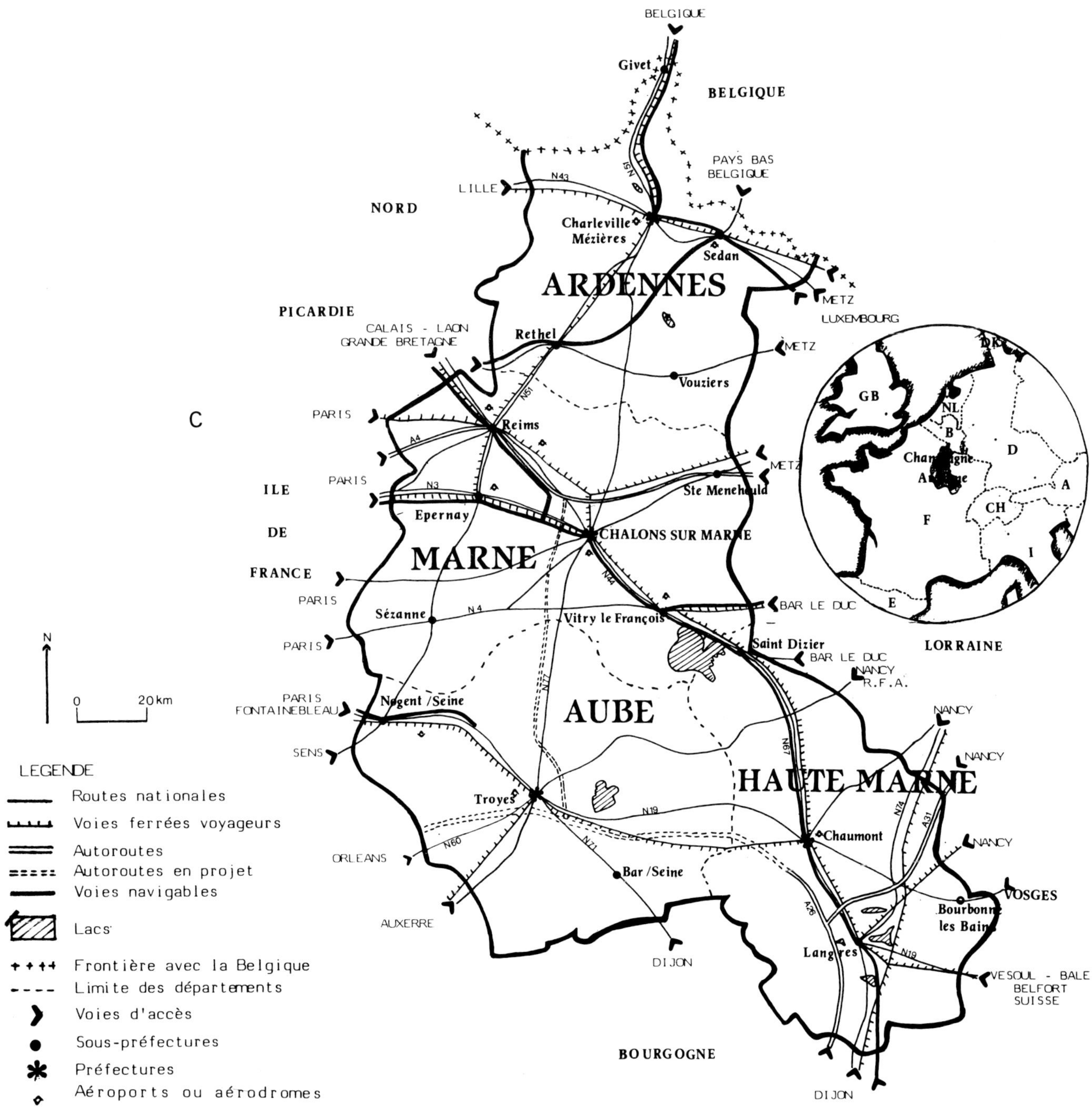

3 D is an information sheet about boating holidays in Ireland.

- **a** Which river is mentioned?
- **b** Where is the marina situated?
- **c** Name one facility you would find there.
- **d** How do you learn about handling the boat?
- **e** Name three safety items on the houseboat.
- **f** What other things would you find on board?
- **g** For whom is this type of holiday not recommended?

DÉCOUVREZ L'IRLANDE EN NAVIGANT SUR LE SHANNON. D

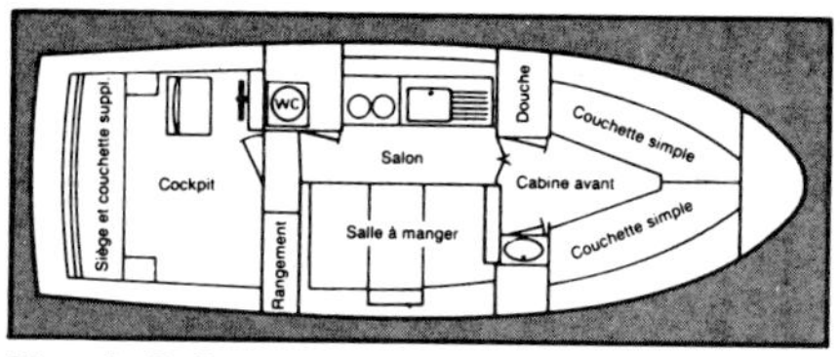

Plan du Ballykeeran House boat.

Découvrez l'Irlande d'une façon inhabituelle en navigant sur le Shannon, une succession de magnifiques lacs.

La marina de base est située a Ballykeeran près d'Athlone. Elle possède un centre de ravitaillement, un parking gratuit, etc.

Les instructions de pilotage vous seront données avant votre départ.

Une assurance au tiers avec franchise (Irl. £ 100 à £ 150) est comprise. Une caution de Irl. £ 100 à £ 150 vous sera demandée avant votre séjour et restituée à votre retour après état des lieux.

Le carburant utilisé est à payer sur place.

Les house boats présentent toutes les normes de sécurité (bouée, gilets et dinghy de sauvetage, boîte de premiers secours, etc.). Ils sont équipés en ustensiles de cuisine et en couchage (draps et couvertures) ainsi qu'en installation sanitaire.

Ce type de séjour n'est pas recommandé pour les enfants en bas âge.

4 E, F and **G** offer ideas for short holiday breaks in England.

E

LA JOURNÉE À DOUVRES OU FOLKESTONE

La formule la moins chère pour découvrir l'Angleterre :

Notre formule comprend :

- La traversée maritime aller-retour (départ avant 11 heures, retour en France avant minuit) le jour de votre choix, depuis Calais ou Boulogne.
- Journée libre à Folkestone ou Douvres.

– ADULTE .... **110 F**

– ENFANT (4 à – 14 ans) .... **76 F**

La journée à Douvres ou Folkestone

- **a** To which English ports are French passengers taken and from which ports might they leave France?
- **b** At what time would they leave France and when would they arrive back?
- **c** What would be the total cost for two adults, one child aged eight and one aged 15?

F

	Avec le bus	Avec le train
1 JOUR à LONDRES	**192 F**	**210 F**
ou à **CANTERBURY**		avec le train **140 F**

Notre formule comprend :

- La traversée maritime aller-retour depuis Calais ou Boulogne (départ conseillé avant 8 h 30, retour en France impératif avant minuit).
- Le parcours ferroviaire ou en bus jusqu'à Londres, ou en train jusqu'à Canterbury (voir schéma des correspondances au dos. Les trains sont fréquents et réguliers).

	ADULTE	ENFANT 4 à – 14 ans
CANTERBURY	140	96
LONDRES avec le bus	192	130
LONDRES avec le train	210	126

Jour à Londres ou à Canterbury

- **a** How much would the same family pay for a rail visit to Canterbury?
- **b** When would they have to leave France to make this trip?
- **c** What two modes of travel are available to London and Canterbury?

Séjour libre en Angleterre

- **a** How long could a French person stay in England on this trip?
- **b** What would it cost three adults, taking the Calais route?

G

SÉJOUR LIBRE EN ANGLETERRE
JUSQU'À 2 JOURS 1/2 à partir de... **176 F**

Cette formule comprend :
- La traversée maritime aller-retour, depuis Calais ou Boulogne (sans restriction de navire).
- Le séjour libre en Angleterre jusqu'à 2 jours 1/2 (60 heures).

– Via Calais	Adulte : **186 F**	Enfant (4 à – 14 ans) : **112 F**
– Via Boulogne	Adulte : **176 F**	Enfant (4 à – 14 ans) : **88 F**

Staying in gîtes

1 Study the list of abbreviations in the left-hand column below and match them up with the jumbled English words on the right.

Autres conforts		**Other facilities**
st	studio	one-roomed flat with bedroom and kitchen
ch	chambre	living room separate from kitchen
c	cuisine	garage
ss	salle de séjour indépendante de la cuisine	enclosed garden
sc	salle de séjour comportant un coin cuisine	fireplace
wc	WC intérieures	kitchen
fr	eau chaude sur évier	gîte in ground floor flat
gar	garage	already rented for '88
abr	simple abri couvert	hot water
ter	terrasse	television
bal	balcon	open for weekends
tc	jardin ou terrain clos	cover for car
t	terrain non clos	balcony
che	cheminée	terrace
TV	télévision	inside WC
la	ouvert toute l'année	bedroom
fs	ouvert en fin de semaine	open all year
X	gîte déjà loué pour 1988	living-room with kitchen

2 **A** is an advertisement for a gîte. Read the information and look back at the list in question 1. Then answer the questions:

- **a** How many levels/storeys does the house have?
- **b** Where could you go for walks?
- **c** Name two sports available nearby.
- **d** What is in the 'salle de séjour'?

A

Gîte de caractère

—sur 2 niveaux comprenant deux corps de bâtiment. Nombreuses possibilités de promenades ou excursions. Pêche, Forêts, Commerces sur place. Centre commercial, tous services, piscine, tennis, équitation, canoë-kayak, ski de fond. Plan d'eau: baignade.
Gîte accueillant 7 personnes. Salle de séjour. (vaste che. ancienne).

3 Look at the information on gîte **B**.
  a With whom would you be sharing this gîte?
  b Name three sporting activities available nearby.
  c Where exactly would the three occupants stay?

4 On finishing a holiday in a French gîte, you are given form **C** to complete.
  a In English, give seven examples of information required in section **A** of the form.
  b On what two things are you asked to comment in the bottom section?

Logement dans la maison du propriétaire sur une exploitation agricole.
Commerçants et services 5km: lac, baignade, voile, tennis, pêche. Sentiers de randonnées pédestres. Fôrets. Gîte au rez-de-chaussée accueillant 3 personnes.

B

C

FICHE D'APPRECIATION
à retourner:
A/ Relais régional des Gîtes—22 bd Paoli

Nom du locataire: ....

Profession: ....

ADRESSE du locataire: ....
....

Nom du Propriétaire du Gîte ....

ADRESSE: ....

PÉRIODE de location: ....

Pris de location: .... par semaine.

Avez-vous déjà utilisé la formule des Gîtes de France: OUI – NON:

Combien de fois? ....

Par quelle voie d'information avez-vous entendu parler du Mouvement des Gîtes de France:

Presse–radio–télévision–amis–autres ....

QUELLES OBSERVATIONS AVEZ-VOUS A FORMULER en ce qui concerne:

1)–L'accueil de votre hôte ....
....

2)–L'aménagement du gîte: ....
....

Hotel accommodation

1 On holiday with a friend, you come across advertisement **A** while searching for accommodation. Give four details about this hotel.

A

2 While planning a visit to the south of France with some friends you examine list **B**.

a In English, give the facilities available at: the Beach Regency; Mercure 2; Plaza Concorde.

b Name the smallest hotel.

c How much would two people pay for full board in the Meridien Nice for two nights?

d Write a letter in French to the hotel Sofitel-Splendid booking a holiday for three people. You wish to stay one week in July and want 'en suite' facilities. Enquire about the proximity of the beach and evening entertainment.

B

HOTELS		Téléphone	Ouverture	Nombre/ch.	Ch./S. de B.	Ch./C. de T.	Informations générales	Prix tout compris – Chambre – Single Mini-Maxi	Prix tout compris – Chambre – Double Mini Maxi	Prix pension par personne – Mini	Prix pension par personne – Maxi
NICE-06000 (Alpes Maritimes)											
BEACH REGENCY 223, promenade des Anglais ϟ461635	L★★★★	93839151	T.A.	322	322		☎ ⇅ 🍴 🍸 ♿ 🐕 (P) ≈ ▲ 💼 ⁞ DC CB AE E TV ⊛	500/1000	600/1200	360	
MERIDIEN NICE 1, Promenade des Anglais ϟ470361	L★★★★	93822525	"	314	314		☎ ⇅ 🍴 🍸 🐕 ≈ ▲ 💼 ⁞ DC CB AE E TV ⊛	700/1300	700/1300	385	
NEGRESCO, 37, prom. des Anglais ϟ460040	L★★★★	93883951	"	150	150		☎ ⇅ 🍴 🍸 🐕 (P) ▲ 💼 ⁞ DC CB AE E TV ⊛	1010/1800	1010/1800		
GRAND HOTEL ASTON 12, av. Félix-Faure ϟ470290	★★★★	93806252	"	160	160		☎ ⇅ 🍴 🐕 💼 ⁞ DC CB AE E TV ⊛				
HOLLIDAY INN 179, BD. RENé CASSIN ϟ970202	★★★★	93839192	"				☎ ⇅ 🍴 🍸 ♿ 🐕 (P) ≈ 💼 ⁞ DC CB AE E TV ⊛	350/660	490/770		
LA PEROUSE, 11, quai Rauba Capeu ϟ461411	★★★★	93623463	"	65	65		☎ ⇅ 🍸 🐕 (P) ≈ ▲ 💼 ⁞ DC CB AE E TV ⊛	300/700	360/950		
MERCURE 2, r. Halevy ϟ970656	★★★★	93823088	"	124	124		☎ ⇅ 🍸 🐕 ▲ 💼 DC CB AE TV ⊛	340/470	380/580		
PARK-HOTEL 6, av de Suède ϟ970176	★★★★	93878025	"	145	145		☎ ⇅ 🍴 🍸 ♿ 🐕 ▲ 💼 ⁞ DC CB AE E TV	360/500	500/630	45/560	
PLAZA CONCORDE 12, av. de Verdun ϟ460979	★★★★	93878041	"	200	200		☎ ⇅ 🍴 🍸 🐕 ▲ 💼 ⁞ DC CB AE E TV ⊛ VID	380/600	480/850	685/905	
SOFITEL-SPLENDID, 50, bd Victor-Hugo ϟ460938	★★★★	93886954	"	128	128	128	☎ ⇅ 🍴 🍸 🐕 (P) ≈ 💼 ⁞ DC CB AE E TV ⊛	450/550	600/800	200	
WESTMINSTER-CONCORDE, 27, prom. des Anglais ϟ460872	★★★★	93882944	"	110	110		☎ ⇅ 🍴 🍸 🐕 ▲ 💼 ⁞ DC CB AE E TV	500/700	700/900		

LÉGENDE DES ABRÉVIATIONS

T.A. = Toute l'année.
☎ = Téléphone dans les chambres.
⇅ = Ascenseur.
▲ = Bord de mer ou de lac.
(P) = Parking.
≈ = Piscine.
🍸 = Mini-Bar.
🍴 = Restaurant.
⊛ = Air conditionné.
♿ = Chambres accessibles aux handicapés physiques.
🐕 = Chiens admis.
💼 = Travail avec agences de voyages.
⁞ = Salon pour séminaires.
TV = Chambre avec télévision.
E AE DC CB = Cartes de crédit.
🏠 = Logis de France.
ϟ = Télex.
△ = Altitude.
(aide) = Avec aide.
VID = Vidéo.

LES PRIX SONT INDIQUÉS EN FRANCS FRANÇAIS

3 While staying in a hotel you notice leaflet **C** in your room:
- **a** What three services are offered?
- **b** How exactly would you obtain each one?

4 Notice **D** appears on the wall of a hotel. Read it carefully and answer these questions:
- **a** What service is offered here?
- **b** What do you dial to obtain the service?
- **c** What must you do to change the time of alarm?

5 Your Dad writes away for information on a hotel. Among the literature he receives is **E**, a 'description générale'. Look at it carefully:
- **a** When exactly was the hotel opened?
- **b** How big is the parking area?
- **c** What facilities are available for children?
- **d** Name two outdoor sports.
- **e** List six things that are standard facilities in all rooms.

C

Pour appeler un numéro extérieur:
Faire le 'O' et composer votre numéro

Pour appeler la réception:
Pour tous renseignements, composer le '9'

Pour savoir si vous avez un message:
Décrocher puis raccrocher votre combiné.
La réception vous rappellera.

NOTICE D'UTILISATION

D

Pour vous réveiller:

Votre chambre est équipée d'un réveil automatique programmable par téléphone.

Composer le '1', attendre le 'BIP', puis numéroter votre heure de réveil qui comportera IMPERATIVEMENT 4 CHIFFRES. Un second 'BIP' vous confirmera l'enregistrement de votre demande.

Exemple: 8h 15 composer 0.8.1.5.

Pour modifier votre heure de réveil:

Après avoir raccroché, renouveler la programmation de la nouvelle heure.

E

Date d'ouverture de l'hôtel - décembre 1972

LES EXTERIEURS

Terrain de 20 000m^2

Parking extérieur gratuit de 2000m^2

Piscine extérieure de 100m^2

Jardin de 7000m^2 avec aires de jeux pour les enfants, 3 courts de tennis, mini-golf, tir à la carabine, et bicyclettes

Terrasse de 650m^2 avec possibilité de repas:
* 100 personnes assises
* 500 personnes debout (cocktail)

Barbecue, chaises longues, parasols

L'INTERIEUR

Air conditionné dans tous les services généraux

Hall de 160m^2

'Le Grill' ouvert de 7 a 23

Bar de 20 places avec cheminée

2 étages desservis par l'ascenseur

Loisirs dans l'hôtel: jeux électriques, fléchettes, ping-pong, jeux de société

LES CHAMBRES

120 chambres

Air conditionné

1 lit double + 1 canapé lit

1 vaste plan de travail

Télévision couleur avec télécommande

Circuit vidéo interne

Radio

Réveil automatique

Téléphone relié directement avec l'extérieur

Salle de bains complète avec toilettes individuelles

Courant 220 V

Service en chambre

6 Notice **F** outside a French hotel provides information on rooms and prices:
  a What do you understand by '2NN'?
  b How much is a room with shower and toilet for two people?
  c What would the price be for a room with a bath and toilet for two people?
  d Is breakfast charged separately? If so, how much is it?
  e What is on offer for 120 francs?
  f In French, book a single room with a shower.
  g In French, book a room for three people with shower and toilet.

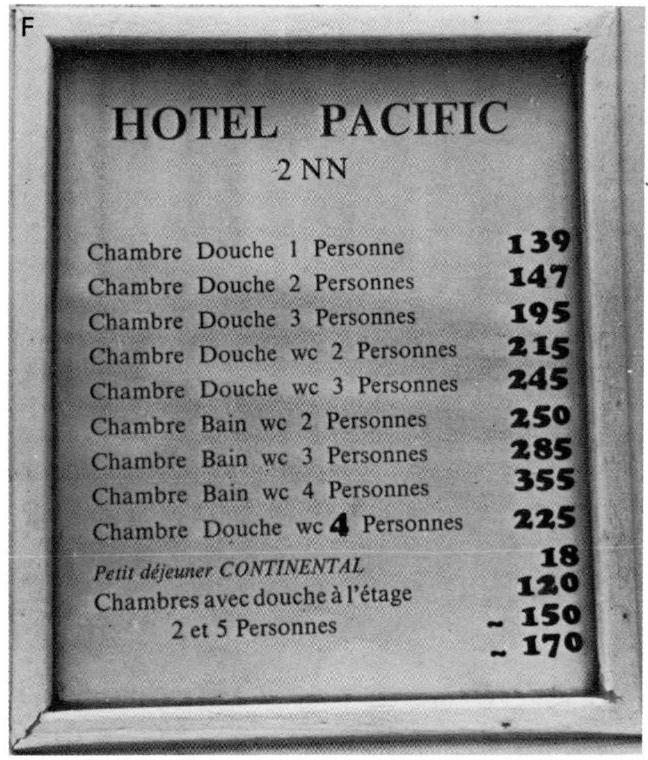

Camping

1 Here are some symbols from a French camping guide. Match up the illustrations with the French words on the left.

Alimentation sur le camp
Réservation
Centre équestre
Plage
Jeux pour enfants
Golf miniature
Toute l'année
Location de bicyclette
Piscine
Restaurant
Accessible aux handicapés
Bord de rivière
Golf
Camping ombragé
Sports nautiques
Plats cuisinés
Tennis
Plan d'eau aménagé
Branchement électrique pour caravanes
Pêche en rivière
Prise d'eau pour caravanes
Location de caravanes, tentes ou bungalows sur le camp

2 You approach a campsite and see notice **A**. How much would it be for a family of two adults, a child of five, one dog and a car to stay the night?

A **CAMPING MUNICIPAL**

Par campeur .... 3.30 F
Par voiture .... 2.0 F
Emplacement .... 3.0 F

½ tarif pour enfants en dessous de 7 ans.   Chiens gratuits.

Emergencies

Signs

1 The warning signs in **A** are often found in factories and workshops. Match them up with the French words below, then explain, in English, what they mean.

risque d'explosion
risque d'électrocution
tête de mort, risque d'intoxication
risque de feu
danger

2 Look at sign **B**.

a Near which French town would this sign be found?
b What potential hazard is nearby?
c What does the sign say about people entering the building?
d What should be done in the event of an emergency?
e What two things are forbidden?

3 Signs **C**, **D** and **E** are found on beaches in France. In English, explain what each of them means.

A

B

C

D

E

4 You spot notice **F** on a French beach. What exactly does each colour of flag tell you?

DRAPEAU VERT en haut du mât: baignade surveillée, absence de danger

DRAPEAU JAUNE ORANGE: baignade surveillée mais dangereuse

DRAPEAU ROUGE: interdiction de se baigner

F

G

5 Who are the men in **G**. What is their job?

6 Where would you find sign **H** and at whom is it aimed? What orders is it giving?

H

Bûcherons !

Chasseurs !

Attention au feu...

Ne fumez pas en forêt

7 Notice **I** is often found in places of work such as offices and factories. How would you explain it to a friend who does not understand French?

- **a** What is the first thing you are told?
- **b** When contacting the fire brigade, what two things must you do?
- **c** What are you advised to do while you wait for the fire brigade to arrive?
- **d** What does the notice say about gas and electricity?
- **e** How would you be able to breathe fresh air in a fire?

I

EN PRÉSENCE D'UN FEU

Ne vous affolez pas et alertez immédiatement les sapeurs-pompiers. Soyez clair dans votre appel et précisez la nature du sinistre. En attendant l'arrivée des secours, utilisez les moyens d'extinction à votre disposition (extincteurs, sable, couverture, etc.). Coupez les compteurs de gaz et d'électricité. Baissez-vous pour éviter l'intoxication; l'air frais est près du sol.

Emergency services

1 Notice **A** tells people how to contact the fire brigade.

- **a** People with telephones can summon help in two ways. What are they?
- **b** If you dial 18, what will you hear first?
- **c** How long will you have to wait for direct communication with the fire brigade?

A

COMMENT APPELER LES SAPEURS-POMPIERS ?

Si vous avez le téléphone, deux possibilités s'offrent à vous :

— Chiffrer le **18.** Vous entendrez d'abord un disque qui répètera 2 à 3 fois « Vous avez demandé les Sapeurs-Pompiers, ne quittez pas ! ». Après quoi (10 secondes environ), vous serez en liaison avec les Sapeurs-Pompiers.

— Composer le numéro d'appel à 7 chiffres de la caserne de Sapeurs-Pompiers dont dépend votre domicile, éventuellement celui de l'une des casernes voisines.

B

EN CAS D'ACCIDENT GRAVE

Tout en assurant un minimum de protection :

1. Appelez ou faites appeler les secours : selon le cas, gendarmerie (campagne) ou police (ville), si vous le voulez médecin, ambulance, sapeurs-pompiers...
2. Pour secourir, rappelez-vous que, pratiquement, il n'y a que deux urgences; mais ce sont des urgences pour lesquelles il n'y a pas une seconde à perdre :
   — l'hémorragie, et
   — l'arrêt respiratoire.
   La première chose à faire est donc de vérifier que l'accidenté :
   — ne saigne pas, et
   — respire.
3. Etendez le blessé :
   — sur le dos, s'il a sa connaissance,
   — sur le côté, s'il est sans connaissance.
4. Tenez-le au chaud, sans trop le réchauffer (couvertures).
5. Ne lui donnez rien à boire.

2 **B** gives French people five pieces of useful information should they come across a serious accident.

- **a** Which sorts of people/organisations should you call to an accident?
- **b** What are the two most urgent situations referred to?
- **c** How would you place an injured person if he or she were: conscious? unconscious?
- **d** In English, explain what you understand by instructions 4 and 5.

3 **C** has further tips on how to summon the emergency services.

- **a** Should you give an injured person something to drink?
- **b** How should you warn other traffic that an accident has occurred?

C

Avant de toucher à un blessé rappelez-vous ceci—faites prévenir les secours (ne jamais lui donner à boire)
Signaler l'accident dans les deux sens de la circulation à 100 m environ de l'accident, à l'aide de triangles réflectorisés ou voitures avec feux de détresse, au bord de la chaussée et non sur le bas côté; jamais dans un virage.

Giving First Aid

A

LE THORAX ET L'ABDOMEN NE SE SOULEVENT PAS AYEZ LE RÉFLEXE DU BOUCHE-A-BOUCHE

Retirez avec le doigt les corps étrangers (caillots, fragments d'os, dentier déplacé ...), qui obstrueraient la gorge, SOULEVEZ LA NUQUE.
RENVERSEZ LA TETE EN ARRIERE tout en tirant doucement sur elle. OPÉREZ LENTEMENT afin d'éviter d'aggraver une possible fracture des vertèbres du cou. UNE MAIN APPUIE FORTEMENT SUR LE SOMMET DE LA TETE, L'AUTRE SOULEVE LE MENTON dont la pointe doit être dirigée vers le haut.
Placez votre bouche largement ouverte sur celle de la victime en appuyant fortement afin d'éviter les fuites d'air. Pour la même raison, fermez les narines en y appuyant la joue fortement ou pincez-les avec la main qui maintient la tête renversée.
SOUFFLEZ FORT. La poitrine doit se soulever.
ENLÉVEZ VOTRE BOUCHE SANS BOUGER LES MAINS. La poitrine s'affaisse.
Recommencez une QUINZAINE DE FOIS PAR MINUTE. Le mieux est de vous guider sur votre propre respiration.

BOUCHE-A-BOUCHE
Stade 1. - mettre la tête en hyperextension.
Insuffler dans la bouche.
Surveiller la poitrine.

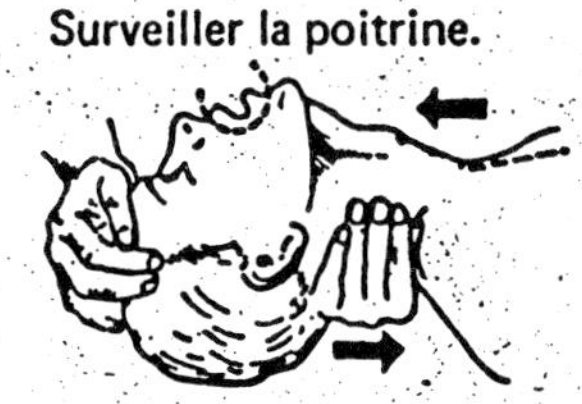

BOUCHE-A-NEZ
Stade 1. - ou mettre la tête en hyperextension en fermant la bouche.
Insuffler par le nez.

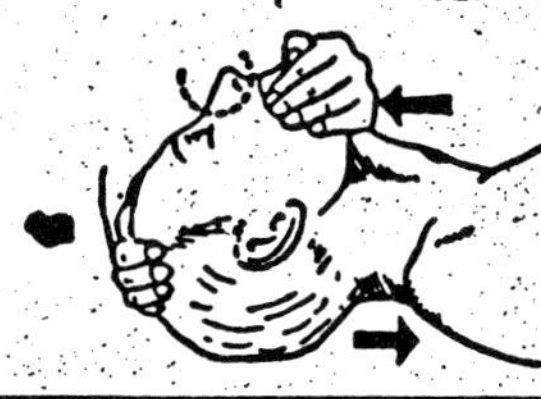

1 Notice **A** appears in a French handbook on First Aid.
- **a** What do you understand by the expression 'bouche-à-bouche'?
- **b** Why should you check inside the patient's mouth?
- **c** If you blow hard, what would you expect to occur?
- **d** How many times a minute should you carry out the procedure?

2 Read the instructions in **B** and answer the following questions.
- **a** What exactly are you advised to do if you suspect a fracture: in the upper part of the body? in the lower part of the body?
- **b** When must a person not be moved?
- **c** Explain fully what has to be done with an unconscious patient.

EN CAS DE FRACTURE

B

La victime a un membre impotent, douloureux, déformé (fracture possible) :

Immobilisez sur place
— le membre supérieur : avec une écharpe,

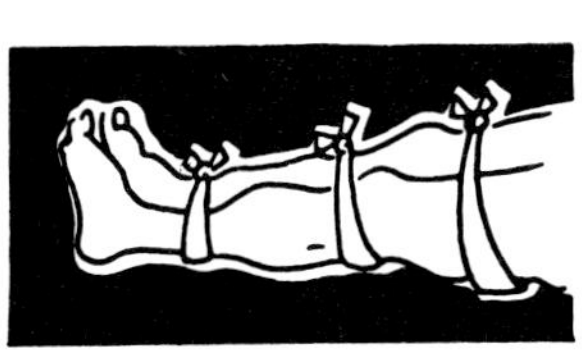

— le membre inférieur : en le liant au membre sain.

Si la victime ayant reçu un choc violent au dos, ne peut pas bouger une jambe, un bras (fracture de la colonne vertébrale possible) :
— Ne la remuez pas;
— Attendez l'arrivée des secours.

La victime a perdu connaissance :

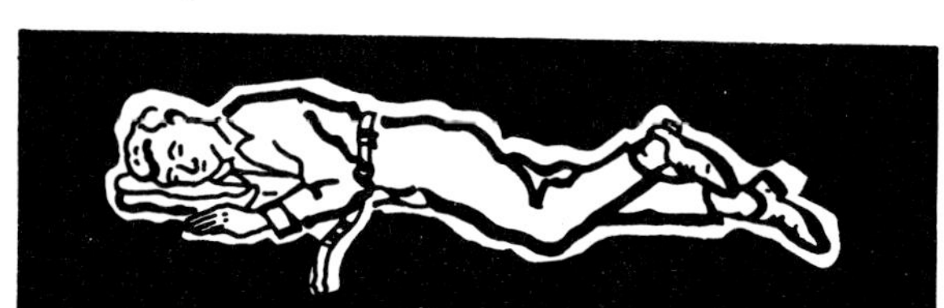

— Couchez-la sur le côté, tête basse, un genou fléchi pour assurer la stabilité. Vêtements desserrés;
— N'essayez pas de la faire boire.

3 In France, ambulances may belong to private organisations or to the local fire brigade. Vehicle **C** is operated by a private concern. What feature is added for the comfort of patients?

C

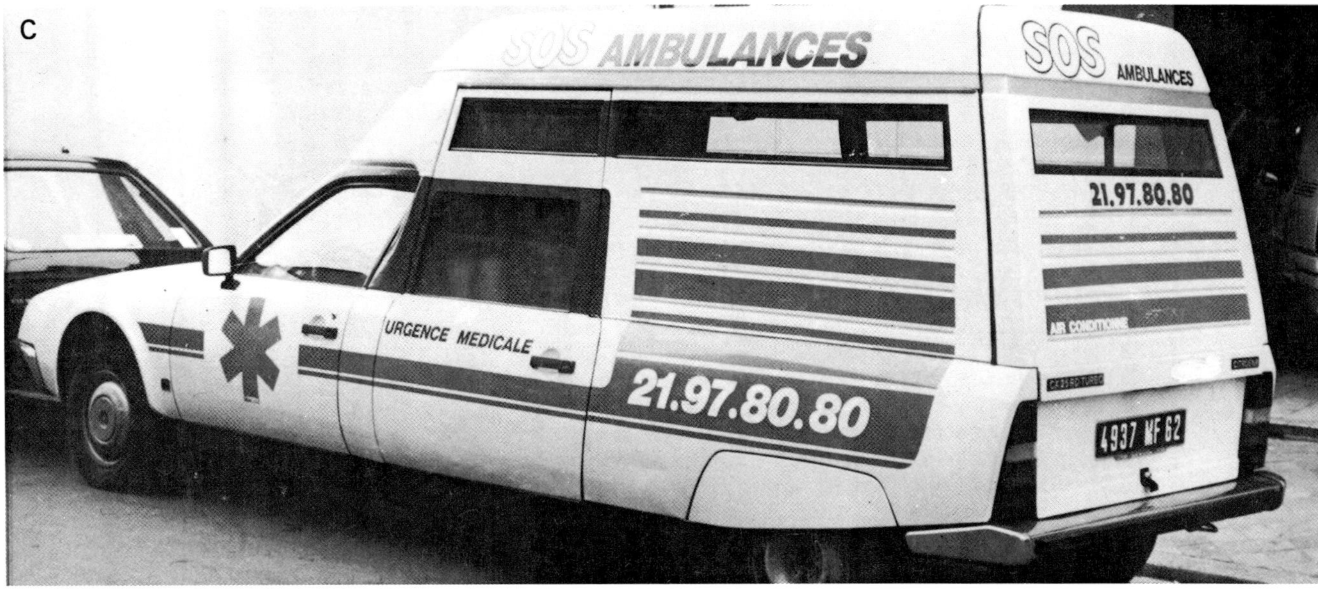

Avoiding accidents

1 **A** is designed to help motorists who are involved in accidents.

- **a** Once an accident has occurred, what two things should you do to prevent further accidents?
- **b** Where should warning triangles be placed? Why?

A

PROTÉGER

Il faut, avant tout, éviter un nouvel accident ou une aggravation de celui qui a eu lieu. Pour cela :

- Coupez le contact sur chaque véhicule accidenté ou, mieux, débranchez la batterie.
- Postez à 100 mètres, dans les deux sens, une personne faisant des signaux de ralentissement (lumineux la nuit).

ou, mieux encore, posez des triangles de sécurité.

Vous avez toujours intérêt à posséder au moins un de ces triangles à bord de votre voiture, en cas de crevaison la nuit, par exemple.

IL NE FAUT JAMAIS poser les triangles ou faire signe de ralentir à MOINS DE 100 MÈTRES du lieu de la collision, ce afin de permettre aux autres automobilistes de ralentir à temps et de s'arrêter avant les obstacles.

2 Read the instructions about 'noyades' in **B** and answer these questions:
   a Where do most accidents occur: for children under four? for children over four?
   b In which season do most incidents take place?
   c What are you told about accidents involving children under four?
   d What could happen if a child goes into cold water straight after a meal?

3 **C** contains six suggestions on how to prevent accidents common to children. Explain the advice given in 1, 2 and 3.

B

Noyades

Les circonstances

Les noyades sont en France, après les accidents de la route, la cause la plus fréquente d'accidents mortels chez l'enfant. Les circonstances varient selon l'âge.
Pour les « grands » au-dessus de 3 ou 4 ans, elles arrivent souvent lorsqu'ils pratiquent un sport. Elles sont plus fréquentes en été.
Pour les petits enfants (moins de 4 ans) la noyade est un accident domestique. Ils peuvent se noyer dans une très faible profondeur d'eau. Ils tombent la tête la première, ne peuvent se relever et meurent noyés dans 20 cm d'eau.

L'hydrocution

La cause habituelle de la noyade est l'inondation du poumon par l'eau. Mais l'arrêt respiratoire peut être provoqué par la simple immersion — même partielle — dans l'eau froide, surtout pendant la digestion. D'où l'interdiction de se baigner moins de trois heures après la fin d'un repas copieux.
L'hydrocution peut avoir bien d'autres causes. Elle peut en particulier être consécutive à un bain d'eau froide pris à jeun ou dans un état de fatigue prononcée.

L'arrêt respiratoire

Une interruption respiratoire brutale peut aussi survenir chez des sujets qui, en se baignant, « boivent la tasse » et envoient de l'eau dans leur trachée. Cette petite quantité d'eau, insuffisante pour inonder complètement les poumons, déclenche pourtant un réflexe de suffocation qui peut être suivi, dans bien des cas, d'une perte de connaissance et d'une noyade.
Tous ces accidents peuvent survenir même chez de bons nageurs. C'est la raison pour laquelle il ne faut jamais laisser quelqu'un se baigner seul.

C

POUR PREVENIR L'ACCIDENT — 6 commandements

1  Apprenez à nager à votre enfant le plus tôt possible.

2  Apprenez-lui dès qu'il a 3 ou 4 ans à mettre la tête sous l'eau et à retenir sa respiration.

3 

Ne forcez jamais un enfant à entrer brutalement dans l'eau. Ne le laissez pas se baigner après un repas et un échauffement prolongé au soleil.

4  Ne laissez jamais un enfant se baigner seul, même s'il nage très bien.

5  Ne laissez pas un enfant de moins de cinq ans seul près d'une pièce d'eau.

6  Pas de baquets remplis d'eau dans les jardins fréquentés par des petits enfants.

EN CAS D'ACCIDENT — En attendant le médecin

- Appelez immédiatement les pompiers.
- Prenez l'enfant par les pieds et maintenez-le cinq secondes la tête en bas.
- Immédiatement après, commencez la respiration artificielle par le bouche-à-bouche. Ne cessez qu'à l'arrivée des secours, en vous faisant relayer au besoin.

4 The French authorities provide useful information like **D** and **E** on how to prevent serious fires and how to tackle small incidents. Study the extracts carefully and try to answer these questions.

a In the case of 'un feu sec', state one way in which you would fight the fire.

b In 'un feu gras' what are you told about water? What should you do with furniture?

c During a camping holiday the person in the next tent sets fire to her hair while she is doing some cooking in the open. According to the document, what should you do?

d What is the greatest danger for a person whose clothes catch fire? Which part of the body should you protect first?

e Should firemen always be called to chimney fires?

D

CAS PARTICULIERS :

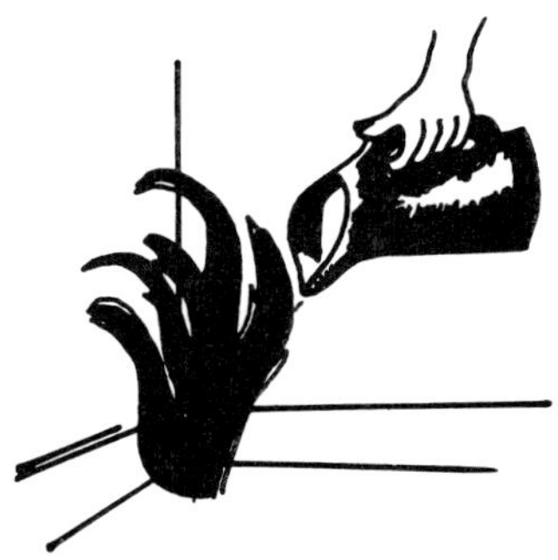

1. **Feu sec :**

   Attaquez avec de l'eau à la base des flammes (comme dit plus haut) ou couvrez l'objet enflammé avec une couverture ou un linge mouillé, ou encore battez le feu avec un balai ou un linge mouillé.

2. **Feu gras (huile, essence) :**

   N'utilisez pas d'eau. Si le liquide est dans un récipient, couvrez celui-ci (couvercle, linge, sciure de bois, etc.). Si le liquide enflammé est à terre, ne vous affolez pas.

   Ecartez d'abord les meubles. L'essence s'éteindra avant que le plancher ne prenne feu.

3. **Feu à des gants que l'on a mis pour les nettoyer à l'essence :**

   Ne vous dégantez pas. Enroulez vos mains dans un linge et pressez, ou si vous le pouvez, plongez vos mains gantées dans un seau d'eau.

4. **Feu aux cheveux :**

   Serrez-les dans une serviette mouillée et mettez la tête sous le robinet.

5. **Feu aux vêtements :**

   Quand les vêtements d'une personne ont pris feu, le grand danger est qu'elle respire les flammes. C'est la cause essentielle des morts si fréquentes dans ce cas. Donc, enveloppez d'abord la tête de la victime. Empêchez la personne de courir, jetez-la à terre et enroulez-la dans une étoffe, pour étouffer les flammes.

6. **Feu de cheminée :**

   Coupez le tirage en baissant le rideau de cheminée ou en fermant la clé du poêle. Appelez toujours les pompiers, même si le feu semble éteint.

E

Emergency situations

1 Accident **A** took place at a:
  a Passage souterrain
  b Passage protégé
  c Passage à niveau
  d Parking gratuit?

2 **B** is a dramatic account written by a French fireman who actually took part in the rescue and fire fighting operation.
  a When exactly was the alarm raised and where was the fire?
  b How many fire engines were sent at first?
  c Describe what the firemen saw when they reached the fire.
  d What do you understand by 'le porte-lance'?
  e Why was there a need to ventilate the shop?
  f Give one example of the damage caused.
  g Where had the blaze started?

Incendie dans un magasin d'électro-ménager

Dans la nuit du 27 au 28 janvier à 0h 40, la sonnerie téléphonique a retenti, le stationnaire a décroché: "Allô les pompiers, venez vite, il y a le feu au magasin ELECTROLUX dans la rue du quartier".

Le standardiste a donné l'alerte et a fait partir un F.P.T. (Fourgon Pompe Tonne) et l'E.P.A. 30 (échelle pivotante automatique 30m.). Il a prévenu également la police.

En arrivant sur les lieux, les pompiers ont vu des flammes sortir par la porte et beaucoup de fumée s'en dégager.

Aussitôt le chef du détachement a donné l'ordre d'établir la L.D.T. (Lance du dévidoir tournant); une fois la lance établie, le porte-lance a attaqué le feu.

Au bout d'un moment, nous avons pu pénétrer dans le magasin afin de terminer l'extinction qui avait été entreprise. En même temps il a fallu aérer le local au-dessus car il était envahi par la fumée.

Il y avait beaucoup de dégâts, les appareils électriques qui n'avaient pas brûlé, avaient fondu par la chaleur, coup classique dans un incendie.

Le feu avait apparemment pris dans l'armoire électrique qui se trouvait dans le magasin. Il ne restait plus qu'à déblayer, car il n'y a pas d'extinction complète sans déblayage.

C

3 Read account **C** of a road traffic accident and answer these questions:

- **a** Where was the accident and what are you told about the place?
- **b** In addition to firemen who else attended?
- **c** What nationality was the driver and how was the vehicle positioned?
- **d** What did the firemen do first?
- **e** What were the driver's injuries and where was he taken?
- **f** What rôle was played by the police?
- **g** How did the firemen prevent any pollution occurring?
- **h** What did they do with the lorry and how were they assisted?

Accident de la circulation

Le 16 juin

Le standard a reçu un appel concernant un accident de la circulation au carrefour d'Elange.

Ce carrefour est un véritable point noir pour les usagers de la route, il se trouve à la sortie de l'autoroute Luxembourg/Thionville.

Nous sommes donc partis avec le F.S.R.L. (Fourgon de Secours Routier Lourd) et le S.A.M.U. (Secours d'Aide Médicale d'Urgence) dont un médecin fait partie de l'équipe.

Arrivés à ce fameux carrefour, il y avait un semi-remorque immatriculé en Belgique couché sur le flanc en travers de la chaussée.

De suite, nous avons dégagé le conducteur du camion qui avait perdu connaissance, dû à un choc qu'il avait reçu à la tête.

Une fois dégagée, la victime fut prise en charge par le S.A.M.U., le médecin lui prodiguait les premiers soins avant de l'évacuer vers l'hôpital.

Pendant ce temps, la police s'est occupée de la circulation.

Comme il y avait une fuite de gas-oil du réservoir, il fallait éviter une pollution terrestre, pour cela nous avons placé une écope reliée à des tuyaux pour récupérer le gas-oil dans une poubelle plastique à l'autre extrémité.

Ensuite il fallait procéder au déchargement de la remorque avant de pouvoir la relever, pour cela nous avons fait appel à une grue.

C'est une opération qui est assez longue, à cause du déchargement.

Writing letters

Postcards

1 Marc sends postcard **A** to his friend René. Read what he says and answer these questions:

- **a** When will his holiday finish?
- **b** What has the weather been like?
- **c** Name one activity Marc has done.
- **d** Where is the hotel he's staying at and who did he meet there?
- **e** What does Marc do at night?
- **f** What does he eat at noon?
- **g** What does Marc say in the last sentence?

2 Raymond writes card **B** to his friend Monique:

- **a** Where exactly is Raymond staying?
- **b** What does he think of the weather?
- **c** How much does he have to pay for the tent?
- **d** Give two details about the showers.
- **e** Where is the beach?
- **f** Why does Raymond have to stop writing?

A

St. Tropez, le 30 juin

Salut René,

Mes vacances à St Tropez se terminent dans une semaine. Il a fait un temps superbe jusqu'ici et j'ai pu faire du ski nautique et de la plongée.

J'habite un petit hotêl pas cher près du port où je me suis fait de nouveaux amis.

Nous allons en boîte tous les soirs et cela me revient à assez cher, aussi le midi je dois me contenter d'un sandwich. Vivement la rentrée qu'on se repose!

A bientôt

Marc

B

Bonjour Monique,

Dinard, le 20 juillet

Aujourd'hui il pleut sur le camping de Dinard. Nous ne sommes pas gâtés par le temps. Quand je pense que nous payons cette tente 60 francs par jour! Heureusement, les douches sont en bon état et pas trop loin de notre emplacement. La plage est à 500m du camping et malgré tout, nous en avons bien profité. Je te quitte à présent car je dois préparer le dîner (je cuisine sous la tente et ce ne'est pas pratique).

Bises

Raymond

Informal letters

1 Bernard is going to visit his penfriend Florence. In **A** he gives some details of his trip. Imagine you are Florence and you discuss his letter with a friend.

- **a** When did Bernard receive Florence's letter?
- **b** When exactly will he leave Cheshire and how will he reach London?
- **c** Which cross-Channel route will Ben take?
- **d** Give the day and time of his arrival in Boulogne.
- **e** Where does he want Florence to meet him?
- **f** How will Florence recognise Bernard?
- **g** What two questions does he ask in the last paragraph?

2 Letter **B** comes from Lisa who lives in Glasgow and is going to visit Nicole in Nantes:

- **a** How long will she stay in Nantes?
- **b** What did Nicole send her recently?
- **c** What is the date and time of Lisa's proposed arrival?
- **d** Where exactly will Lisa arrive?
- **e** What will she be wearing?
- **f** What does she send Nicole in her letter?
- **g** Give two details about Lisa's appearance.

A

15, Hathersage Way,
Chester,
Cheshire CH3 SUB

le 10 juillet

Chère Florence,

Merci de ta gentille lettre que j'ai reçue la semaine dernière. Je quitterai le Cheshire vendredi matin et je prendrai le train de Londres. Puis j'irai à Douvres et j'arriverai à Boulogne vendredi soir vers 6 heures. Est-ce que tu viendras m'attendre au port? Je porterai un pull vert et un pantalon noir. Où dois-je attendre exactement?

Peut-être que nous irons passer quelques jours au bord de la mer? Moi, j'aime la pêche - et toi?

Réponds-moi vite,

Ton ami,

Bernard

B

94, Gladstone Walk,
Glasgow,
G4 OTL

le 30 juin

Chère Nicole,

Je te remercie de ta dernière lettre m'invitant à passer une semaine chez toi à Nantes. Merci beaucoup pour les photos de ta famille.

J'arriverai le dimanche matin, 20 juillet à la gare par le train de 8h. 30 et je porterai une jupe grise et un pull vert.

Je t'envoie une photo de moi et de ma famille - j'ai les cheveux longs et je porte des lunettes.

En attendant de faire ta connaissance,

Bien à toi,

Lisa

3 Paul comes from Surrey and has sent his penfriend, David, letter **C** in which he talks about his family, school and friends:

- **a** Where was the family photograph taken?
- **b** How many brothers and sisters does Paul have?
- **c** What do Raymond, Roger and Thomas do?
- **d** Give two pieces of information about Paul's school.
- **e** Which subject does he like and which one does he dislike?
- **f** Why does Paul have lots of homework?
- **g** Where do most of his friends live?
- **h** What does he usually do at the weekend?
- **i** What did he do this weekend?
- **j** Why does Paul have to end the letter?

4 Charles is looking forward to visiting his penfriend Hélène in Paris. She takes letter **D** to school to show her friends and they ask the following questions:

- **a** When will Charles come to Paris?
- **b** Where and when will he arrive?
- **c** Does he want Hélène to meet him?
- **d** Where will he stay in France before going to Nice?
- **e** How long does he wish to stay at Hélène's?
- **f** State one thing Charles says about Paris. What does he ask Hélène for?
- **g** What does Charles, as a soccer fan, hope to do in Paris?
- **h** What does Charles want to do at night?

C

19 Faulkner Avenue
Reigate
Surrey
RH2 OEJ

le 2 mars

Cher David,

Merci beaucoup pour ta lettre. Voici une photo de ma famille; nous sommes à la campagne. J'ai trois frères, Raymond, Roger et Thomas et je n'ai pas de soeur. Raymond est agent de police. Roger est au chômage et Thomas va au Lycée de notre ville.

Mon école se trouve en ville et nous sommes 700 élèves. Moi, je n'aime pas les sciences, mais j'aime les maths. J'ai beaucoup de devoirs parce que je dois passer des examens cette année!

La plupart de mes copains habitent près de chez moi et le week-end nous jouons au football.

Ce week-end je suis allé à Brighton avec mes parents. Et toi, que fais tu le week-end?

Bon, je te quitte car je dois aller à l'école.

Salut,

Paul

D

43 Perkin Avenue,
Lincoln, LN8 OEI.

Le 20 juillet.

Chère Hélène,

Merci bien pour tes nouvelles. Je vais arriver à Paris dans deux semaines. J'arriverai à la Gare du Nord à 19H. 30. samedi, 2 août. Est-ce que tu peux venir me voir à la gare?

J'ai l'intention de passer quelques jours à l'auberge de jeunesse, avant d'aller rejoindre des copains à Nice. Est-ce que je peux passer une nuit chez toi?

Paris est une capitale célèbre et il y aura beaucoup à faire. Peux-tu me donner des renseignements sur les spectacles et la vie sociale?

Tu sais bien que je suis un fana de football. Sera-t-il possible d'assister à un match de football à Paris?

Je voudrais aussi aller en boîtz - je suis sûr qu'il y en a beaucoup à Paris.

En attendant le plaisir de te voir,

Ton copain,

Charles..

E

10, route de la Gaude,
54000, Nancy
le 7 juin

54000 Nancy

Cher Darren,

Je te remercie de ta dernière lettre m'invitant à passer quelque temps chez toi à Macclesfield. C'est avec plaisir que j'accepte ton invitation et j'arriverai le 20 juillet à la gare de Macclesfield au train de 20.30. J'espère qu'il n'aura pas de retard. J'aurais un tricot rouge et un pantalon gris.

Mes parents t'invitent chez nous du 3 au 14 août. J'espère que tu vas accepter et que tu me répondras rapidement. Est-ce que tu viendras m'attendre à la gare?

Je quitterai Nancy le 18 juillet et je passerai une nuit à Paris chez ma tante. Puis je prendrai le bateau à Calais.

J'attends ta réponse,

Roland

5 Roland lives in France and has been invited to stay with Darren. In **E** he gives details of his plans.

- **a** Where does Darren live?
- **b** Where and when exactly will Roland arrive?
- **c** What does he hope and what will he be wearing?
- **d** Why are the dates '3rd to 14th August' significant?
- **e** Where does he hope to meet Darren?
- **f** When will Roland leave home and why will he visit Paris?
- **g** From which French port will he sail?
- **h** Imagine you are Darren. Write a reply in about eighty words saying you will meet Roland, and wish him a safe journey.

6 Jacques lives in the south of France and writes letter **F** to Lynda:

- **a** When did he receive her letter?
- **b** When and why does he hope to visit England?
- **c** To which university will Jacques go and what subjects will he study there?
- **d** Who are his favourite English authors?
- **e** What exactly does he say about his preferences in French literature?
- **f** What job would he like?
- **g** In what geographical areas would he like to work?
- **h** Why is Jacques a bit worried at the moment?
- **i** What does he say about French and Chemistry?
- **j** When he writes next time, what does he hope to tell Lynda?

F

121, rue d'Alsace,
06130, Grasse,
Alpes-Maritimes

le 20 juillet

Chère Lynda,

Merci bien pour ta lettre que j'ai reçue hier. J'ai l'intention de venir en Angleterre l'année prochaine. Je veux améliorer ma connaissance de l'anglais, et il faut résider dans un pays anglophone pour maîtriser la langue.

Puis, j'irai à la fac de Nice, où j'étudierai l'anglais, la littérature et le langage. Mes auteurs préférés sont Jane Austen et Dickens. Je lis aussi des romans français, par exemple ceux de Vailland et de Simenon.

Mon ambition est de devenir professeur d'anglais dans le Midi ou dans l'ouest de la France. Je suis un peu inquiet en ce moment car j'attends les résultats du Bac. J'espère que j'obtiendrai de bonnes notes ! Surtout en Français et en Chimie qui sont mes matières principales et donc à plus forts coefficients.

J'espère que la prochaine fois que je t'écrirai, j'aurai de bonnes nouvelles,

Amitiés,

Jacques.

7 In **G**, Michel replies to a letter from Paul.

a What did Paul ask Michel about in a previous letter?

b What would you expect to find at 'Le Stade Rennais'?

c Where exactly is this place?

d Give two details about 'le centre commercial'?

e Name two forms of evening entertainment available.

f What could students do at the weekend in Rennes?

g Give the location of Rennes. Why is this an advantage?

h What two questions are asked by Michel in the last paragraph?

i Imagine you are Paul. Write a reply in French in eighty words saying you hope to visit Rennes next August, and giving details of the date and time of your arrival at Cherbourg.

G

Cher Paul

19, rue Veron
Rennes
Ille-et-Vilaine

le 9 mai

Me voici à Rennes. Tu m'as posé des questions sur ma ville natale. Je vais essayer de répondre à tes questions dans cette lettre.

D'abord, le football. Oui, il y a une équipe professionelle à Rennes, 'Le Stade Rennais'. Le stade est à l'ouest du centre-ville. Récemment elle a remporté plusieurs succès dans la ligue.

Le centre commercial est moderne et très grand - on peut passer toute la journee dans les magasins. Il y a des boîtes de nuit et des clubs de jeunes. Aussi il y a souvent des soirées à la fac le week-end.

Rennes se trouve à 60km du bord de mer, il est donc très facile de faire un tour sur la côte.

Viendras-tu à Rennes en août? Est-ce que tu peux m'écrire, pour me donner la date et l'heure de ton arrivée à Cherbourg... ou au Havre.

A bientôt,

Michel

H

25 Conwy Avenue,
Llandudno,
Gwynedd,
North Wales
le 20 avril

Chère Claudette,

J'ai vu ton annonce dans un journal au collège. J'ai quinze ans et voici une photo de ma soeur et moi. Elle a douze ans et elle est très bavarde!

Llandudno est une ville du Pays de Galles et ma maison se trouve tout près de la plage. C'est une jolie petite ville mais quelquefois je pense que je préférerais la vie dans une grande ville, par exemple Liverpool ou Manchester.

Comme distractions nous avons des boîtes de nuit, une piscine, des cinémas et un théâtre, et pour les sportifs on peut faire de la planche à voile, du tennis et du football.

J'habite ici depuis six ans avec ma famille. Mon père est pompier et ma mère est serveuse; elle travaille beaucoup en été quand on va au bord de la mer pour les vacances.

Ma maison est assez grand avec un grenier et un sous-sol. Nous avons le chauffage central et un grand garage. J'aime regarder la télévision et mes emissions préférées sont les concerts de rock et les variétés.

Ma mère va écrire à ta mère pour lui demander de passer une semaine chez nous en juillet - j'espère que tes parents et toi viendrez en juillet.

J'attends de tes nouvelles, réponds-moi vite,

Ton copain,

Alan

8 Alan sends **H** to a new penfriend:

- **a** How did Alan obtain Claudette's name and address?
- **b** How old is Alan and what does he send Claudette?
- **c** Give two details about Alan's sister.
- **d** Where is Llandudno and where is Alan's house?
- **e** Describe Llandudno and say why Alan refers to Liverpool and Manchester.
- **f** Name three places you could visit at night in Llandudno.
- **g** Give three examples of sporting facilities on offer.
- **h** For how long has Alan lived there?
- **i** What are the occupations of his parents and what is said about his mother's job?
- **j** Give two details about Alan's house.
- **k** Give three ways in which he spends his spare time.
- **l** Why and to whom is Alan's mother going to write?
- **m** This is the first letter Claudette has received from Alan.
  - **i** What sort of things would she write in her reply?
  - **ii** Write a letter from her in French, about one hundred words in length, referring to her home, town, spare time activities and a possible visit to Llandudno. (Watch out for agreements. Remember the letter is from a girl!)

9 Read letter **I** from André to Alison.

- **a** What two things does André say he will describe in the letter?
- **b** What job would he like to have?
- **c** Which is his favourite soccer team and what does he say about it?
- **d** What two questions does André ask in the second paragraph?
- **e** What sport does André not like? What does he like doing?
- **f** Where did he go for the weekend, what things of interest could you find there?
- **g** Name two things you might do in the Amboise area.
- **h** What hobby does André have?
- **i** What two things are you told about Sandra Kim?
- **j** Which does André prefer, the radio or television?
- **k** What question is asked in the last paragraph and what does André tell Alison to do?
- **l** Write a reply in French from Alison, making sure you answer all André's questions in the letter.

I

Chère Alison,   Angers, le 10 octobre

Merci beaucoup pour ta lettre. Dans cette lettre, je vais te parler de mes sports favoris et de mes passe-temps. Je suis fanatique de football et je voudrais être footballeur. Mon équipe favorite est St Etienne et je pense que nous avons la meilleure équipe de football de France!

Le netball est-il ton sport préféré? Vas-tu souvent à la piscine? Moi, je n'aime pas la natation, mais j'aime la vie en plein air. Ce weekend, je suis allé au Camping de Charge près d'Amboise. Cette ville est située au centre de la region des châteaux et des excursions sont organisées en autocar vers Chambord, Loches et Chinon.

Différents centres de distractions se sont crées autour d'Amboise, comportant des aires de pique-nique et des parcours de pêche. Vas-tu souvent à la pêche?

J'aime collectionner les disques et la semaine prochaine il y a ici un concert. Ma chanteuse préférée est Sandra Kim et j'adore son disque 'J'aime la Vie'. Aimes-tu écouter des disques? As-tu déjà assisté à un concert?

Je n'aime pas tellement la radio mais je regarde souvent la télévision, même les concerts de musique classique!

Quels sont tes passe-temps préférés? Raconte-moi vite tout dans ta prochaine lettre,

Ton ami,

André

J

10, Rue de Limoges,
93100, Montreuil,
France.

le 19 décembre

Chère Karen,

Ta dernière lettre était intéressante. Ici en France, on passe la veillée de Noël en famille, c'est à dire les parents et les enfants. On va à la messe de minuit, puis on réveillonne. Généralement on mange des huîtres avec du vin blanc, de la dinde aux marrons et de la "bûche". Dans presque toutes les maisons, il y a un sapin décoré de guirlandes, et de boules multicolores et une crèche. Avant d'aller se coucher chacun laisse une chaussure au pied de sapin (c'est là que le père Noël dépose les cadeaux!) Le jour de Noël toute la famille se réunit, les oncles, les tantes et les cousins pour un grand repas. Si Noël se passe en famille, le Nouvel An se fête plutôt entre amis. On réveillonne de nouveau dans la nuit du 31 décembre au 1er janvier. A minuit, tout le monde s'embrasse et se souhaite une bonne année. Au petit matin on mange la soupe aux oignons et on va se coucher !

A bientôt et joyeux Noël !

Monique

10 Christmas is approaching as Monique drops a line to Karen (**J**), outlining some of the festivities in France.

- **a** What does Monique say about Karen's last letter?
- **b** Explain the expression 'en famille'.
- **c** Where do French people go at midnight on Christmas Eve?
- **d** Name three things that are eaten and give an example of what is drunk.
- **e** Name one thing found in French houses at Christmas.
- **f** What do people do before going to bed?
- **g** State exactly what happens on Christmas Day.
- **h** If Christmas is a family occasion, what happens at New Year?
- **i** What happens from 31st December to the 1st January?
- **j** What is eaten then?
- **k** Reply in French to Monique in one hundred words, describing Christmas and New Year in England and referring to customs, food and presents people receive.

11 Look at letter **K** from Alice to Paul.

- **a** When did she receive his letter and why did she not reply straight away?
- **b** In paragraph two what are we told about a book?
- **c** How exactly can the book be obtained in the USA?
- **d** What question does Alice ask in connection with photographs of villages?
- **e** What is meant by the last paragraph?

12 Anne is upset when she reads Philippe's letter **L**.

- **a** How does Philippe describe the last few weeks?
- **b** How long have they been going out together?
- **c** What excuse does Philippe give for not seeing Anne?
- **d** Who will he see tomorrow and where does she work?
- **e** What piece of advice does he give in the first sentence of the last paragraph?
- **f** What has François said about Anne?
- **g** What does Philippe hope for?
- **h** Write Anne's reply to this letter in eighty words of French. You can be upset, indignant or annoyed.

K

21, rue des Jardins
69003, Lyon
le 14 mai

Cher ami,

J'ai bien reçu ta lettre du 20 avril. Tu m'excuseras de ne répondre que si tardivement, mais des occupations profesionnelles très importantes m'ont empêché d'y répondre plus tôt.

Je te confirme que j'expédie ce jour même un exemplaire du livre que j'ai réalisé sur les villages en France.

Il est possible d'obtenir ce livre aux Etats-Unis par l'intermédiare des LIVRES FRANÇAIS que tu connais certainement.

En ce qui concerne les photographies de villages, pourrais-tu me renseigner sur l'usage que tu comptes en faire?

J'envisage en effet ultérieurement la publication d'un nouvel ouvrage et il serait dommage que ces documents aient déjà fair l'objet d'une diffusion.

Dans l'attente de te lire, je te prie de recevoir, cher Paul, mes amitiés les plus cordiales,

Alice

L

Anne,

Mardi, le 29 juillet

Tu te doutes certainement du contenu de cette letre. Depuis quelques semaines, ça ne marche plus entre nous. Après 6 mois fantastiques passés ensemble quelque chose s'est cassé entre toi et moi et nous n'y pouvons rien.

Nous avons trop de boulot avec l'école et il devient difficile de se voir, surtout avec mon nouveau job à mi-temps. Tu le sais peut-être déjà, je dois voir demain soir une fille qui bosse dans le même magasin que moi. Mais je préfère t'en parler dès maintenant et être franc envers toi.

Voir quelqu'un d'autre m'aidera peut-être à t'oublier. Cela ne sera pas facile pour toi non plus. Tu devrais appeler François. Il t'aime bien et me parle souvent de toi. J'espère en tout cas que nous resterons amis, toi et moi.

Je t'embrasse tendrement,

Ton ami,

Philippe

Formal letters

1 Mrs Alwoodley lives in Hampshire and has written to a French hotel. **A** is the reply she receives.

- **a** When did Mrs Alwoodley send her letter?
- **b** What two things does Guy Galant send her?
- **c** How much would it cost for breakfast, per person, at the Hôtel de la Gare?
- **d** Where exactly is the hotel and how frequent is the métro?
- **e** In French, write Mrs Alwoodley's reply to this letter (in about 100 words). Say you would like to stay for 10 days and there will be two adults and two children under 14 years of age. You are coming by car and want to know if there is a garage. Enquire about the possibility of an evening meal and ask how much deposit is required. Remember to address the letter correctly.

A

Hôtel de la Gare
11, rue de l'Horloge,
75012, Paris

Paris, le 3 mars

Madame H Alwoodley,
51, Mellands Lane,
Basingstoke,
Hampshire. RG22 6PH

Madame,

Suite à votre courrier du 21 courant, nous vous remercions de l'intérêt que vous portez à notre établissement.

Nous vous faisons parvenir les dépliants de notre hôtel ainsi que la carte de notre restaurant.

Nos tarifs en vigueur sont les suivants:

- 336,00 F la chambre simple ou double
- 32,00 F le petit déjeuner par personne

Notre hôtel est situé à 1 km de la station de métro 'Le Guichet'. Il y a des métros tous les 1/4 d'heure en direction St Michel.

Nous restons à votre entière disposition pour tout renseignement complémentaire.

Nous vous prions d'agréer, Madame, l'expression de nos salutations distinguées.

Guy Galant

B

Le Havre, le 2 avril

Hôtel Castelot,
Le Havre,
Seine-Maritime.

Monsieur Albert Evry,
21, rue Lambert,
Paris.

Monsieur,

Nous avons bien reçu votre courrier et nous vous en remercions.

Nous allons essayer de répondre à vos questions bien que vous ne nous ayez pas précisé les dates de votre séjour.

L'hôtel Castelot se trouve à 5 minutes en voiture du golf de La Plage. Nous vous joignons une documentation.

Nous serions heureux de vous recevoir dans notre établissement; à partir de 15 personnes nous vous accorderions le tarif groupe, c'est à dire, en 1/2 pension: 167 F par personne en chambre double.

La location d'une salle vous coûtera 150 F par jour.

Il y a des possibilités d'organiser des excursions, mais cela dépend de la période de l'année.

Nous restons à votre disposition pour tout renseignement complémentaire.

Meilleures Salutations,

Maurice Dunet

2 Monsieur Evry is trying to organise a trip to Le Havre. He wrote to L'Hôtel Castelot and **B** is the reply.

- **a** How long does it take to reach the golf links?
- **b** What is the main advantage of a party booking?
- **c** How much will it cost per person and what sort of accommodation is provided?
- **d** What costs 150 francs?
- **e** Is it possible to go on trips? What factors affect this?
- **f** Write a reply on behalf of Monsieur Evry. Say that 20 golfers wish to stay for two weeks, commencing on 3 August. Point out that you will require 'une salle' for six days. Enquire if the hotel could contact a coach firm to provide transport to the golf links. Ask how much deposit is required.

3 Mr Atherton is considering a holiday in Cannes and he writes letter **C** to a hotel there.

- **a** How did he obtain the Hôtel Panoramer's address?
- **b** When is Mr Atherton thinking of going on holiday?
- **c** For how many people would he like to book a room and what facility does he require?
- **d** What sort of view would the occupants like?
- **e** In the second paragraph Mr Atherton asks a number of questions. Put any four of them into English.
- **f** Write a reply on behalf of the Hôtel Panoramer. In it, say that the hotel is booked for the period in question and that there are no rooms free with the facilities required. Ask if Mr Atherton would like a booking for an alternative date.

C

18, Clevedon Walk,
Shrewsbury,
Shropshire,
SY1 3HJ

Shrewsbury, le 15 avril

Hôtel Panoramer,
8 - 12, rue Bourgogne,
06400, Cannes

Monsieur,

Votre adresse m'a été communiquée par le Syndicat d'Initiative de Cannes et je désirerais savoir s'il vous reste des chambres de libre pour la troisième semaine d'août. J'aimerais réserver une chambre pour trois personnes avec douche et vue sur la mer. Avez-vous quelque chose de libre?

Pourriez-vous m'indiquer dans votre réponse la situation de l'hôtel et le prix des chambres? Pourriez-vous m'indiquer le prix de la pension complète et joindre un modèle de menu? Avez-vous un dépliant de l'hôtel? A quelle distance se trouve la plage?

Dans l'attente de votre réponse, je vous prie d'agréer, Monsieur, l'expression de mes salutations distinguées,

Monsieur Atherton

D

Taunton, le 25 avril

Monsieur Kerr
12 Hanwell Road
Taunton
Somerset
TA2 8LQ

Townsend Thoresen,
41, place d'Armes,
62226, Calais.

Monsieur le Directeur,

Nous avons l'intention de nous rendre en France, voire même en Espagne, au mois de juin prochain. Aussi en arrivant au Havre, nous voudrions louer une voiture pour 15 jours. Nous serons 4 personnes plus les bagages, aussi nous faudrait-il une voiture suffisamment spacieuse, confortable, de même qu'économique. Si possible, nous aimerions louer un Renault automatique, de préférence.

Quel serait le prix pour 15 jours avec quel kilométrage? Devrions-nous verser un accompte? Quel en serait le montant?

De quels papiers devrons-nous nous munir? Et faudrait-il souscrire à une assurance spéciale?

En vous remerciant à l'avance, veuillez agréer, Monsieur le Directeur, l'expression de mes sentiments distingués,

S Kerr

4 In **D**, Mr Kerr enquires about the possibility of hiring a car.

- **a** Which countries does he hope to visit?
- **b** At which cross-Channel port will he arrive, and for how long does he want to hire a car?
- **c** How many people will be going on the holiday?
- **d** What three things must the car have?
- **e** Which precise model does he want?
- **f** What three questions does he ask in paragraph two?
- **g** What does he ask in the next paragraph?
- **h** Reply on behalf of Townsend Thoresen in Calais. Explain that a car can be arranged for June, but you will need to know the exact date required. Insurance will be provided and a current driving licence is essential. The party will be met at the boat. A leaflet giving further details is enclosed.

5 A group of English boys and girls are considering a youth hostel holiday in France. **E** is their letter to a hostel in Caen.

- **a** What information is given in the first paragraph?
- **b** What do they ask in paragraph two?
- **c** State two questions asked in paragraph three?
- **d** What two places does S Tipton ask about, in relation to the location of the hostel?
- **e** You work at Caen Youth Hostel. Send a reply to the letter explaining that there is no room available for the requested period, but there would be vacancies from 11 July. Answer *all* the questions in the letter.

6 Reply to note **F** from Docteur Coudvin, saying that you have changed to another doctor but that you will note the details he has given in his letter.

7 **G** is a letter from the Crédit Agricole Mutuel

- **a** Translate the letter into English
- **b** In French, write a reply of about eighty words, saying that you will contact Monsieur Nemard's secretary and arrange a time for a meeting. Apologise for any inconvenience caused.

E

Macclesfield, le 8 février

Monsieur S Tipton,
6 Dorset Avenue,
Macclesfield,
Cheshire.

Auberge de Jeunesse de Caen,
17, avenue du Château,
14000 Caen.

Monsieur le Directeur de l'Auberge de Jeunesse de Caen,

Nous sommes un groupe de 3 garçons et de 3 filles, et désirerions passer une semaine à votre Auberge en juillet. Avez-vous la possibilité de nous héberger pendant la période du 3 au 10 juillet?

J'aimerais connaître les facilités qu'offre votre Auberge, s'il est possible de laver du linge, s'il y a un foyer avec un téléviseur.

Pourriez-vous aussi me renseigner sur les horaires d'ouverture et de fermeture, sur les heures de repas, ainsi que sur les tarifs pour la nuit avec petit déjeuner. Les sacs de couchage sont-ils fournis?

Quelles sont les activités prévues à Caen pendant la semaine du 3 au 10 juillet? A quelle distance se trouve la gare de l'Auberge et quelle est l'Auberge la plus proche de la vôtre?

Dans l'attente de vous lire, veuillez croire, Monsieur le Directeur, en l'assurance de mes sentiments les meilleurs,

S. Tipton

F

Docteur S Coudvin
3, rue de la Gare
75016, Paris

Paris, le 3 novembre

Monsieur Gaspard
104, rue d'Auby,
Paris.

Cher Monsieur Gaspard,

Je vous prie de bien vouloir prendre connaissance de ma nouvelle adresse -

3, rue de la Gare,
75016, Paris.

Votre dernière visite remontant à six mois, je vous invite à prendre contact avec ma secrétaire afin de convenir d'un nouveau rendez-vous. Mon numéro de téléphone demeure inchangé.

Je permets toutefois de vous le rappeler, à toutes fins utiles.

En espérant vous recevoir bientôt, je vous prie d'agréer, Monsieur, l'expression de mes sentiments les meilleurs.

S. Coudvin

G

Crédit Agricole Mutuel,
17, Rue du Nivernais,
50000 Saint-Lô Cédex 8

Saint-Lô, le 28 janvier

Monsieur Arnaud
28, rue du Petit-Clamart,
75014, Paris

Cher Monsieur,

Apres vérification, votre compte no. 00815196 présentait à la date du 21 janvier un solde débiteur de 13000 francs. J'aimerais avoir avec vous une conversation à ce sujet. Je vous serais reconnaissant de bien vouloir téléphoner à ma secrétaire afin de convenir d'un rendez-vous au plus tôt.

Une liste de vos principaux achats dans les six derniers mois pourrait également m'être précieuse.

En vous remerciant de votre compréhension je vous prie, Monsieur, d'agréer l'expression de mes salutations distinguées.

J Nemard

Fondé de pouvoir.

8 Read letter **H**, from L'Hôtel du Lac.

- **a** What would you get for 720 francs?
- **b** How much extra must you pay for a continental breakfast?
- **c** What facilities are on offer; at 295 francs? at 250 francs?
- **d** What two 'forfaits' are mentioned?
- **e** Would any service charges be paid on the prices shown?
- **f** State in full what is available for the winter of 87/88.
- **g** Imagine you own a hotel. Write a letter in French outlining its facilities, prices and special attractions. (Do not copy out sections from the letter provided)
- **h** Write a letter booking a two-week holiday for 20 netball players at L'Hôtel du Lac. Enquire about training facilities and the opportunity to play against local teams.

H

L'Hôtel du Lac,
Le Touquet,
Pas de Calais

Le Touquet, le 2 mars

Monsieur L. Warwick,
9 Firbank Close,
Bristol,
Avon. BS1 7EU

Monsieur,

Suite à votre lettre du 08 août '86, nous vous remercions de votre intérêt pour l'Hôtel du Lac.

C'est avec plaisir que nous vous communiquons nos disponibilités et conditions spéciales "Groupe":

A/Période du 11 au 17 octobre '87
ou du 21 au 25 octobre '87

Conditions spéciales "Groupe" chambre simple.... 720 FF
chambre double.... 800 FF

Supplément petit déjeuner continental.......... 56 FF
" " " americain............ 115 FF

B/Nous vous proposons également nos forfaits séminaires:
Forfait Exécutif............................ 295 FF
Forfait Affaires............................ 250 FF

Nos forfaits comprennent par jour:
Utilisation gratuite de la salle
Matériel audio-visuel de base
Déjeuner 3 plats (boissons comprises)

Tous nos prix s'entendent nets, taxes et service compris.

Un important programme de rénovation entrepris dès l'hiver 87/88 offre à notre clientèle:

130 chambres et salles de bains entièrement renovées.
Une salle de banquet style "Belle Epoque" accueillant 200 personnes (banquets) à 400 personnes (cocktail).
Un Restaurant Gastronomique.
De nouvelles salles de réunion aménagées pour des séminaires et conférences de 15 à 140 personnes.
Un restaurant et Bar de la Plage d'une capacité maximale de 180 personnes (banquets).

Veuillez trouver ci-joint une brochure complète sur notre hôtel.

Nous restons à votre disposition pour toute information complémentaire.

Dans l'attente de vous lire, veuillez croire, Monsieur, à l'expression de nos sentiments les meilleurs.

Marcel Gothard

9 You are an employee of *World Wide Press.* Because you understand French, you are asked to deal with letter **I**, from Monsieur Grenier.

 a Translate the letter into English.

 b In French, write a short reply (about eighty words).

10 Translate letter **J** from Alain Terieur and write a suitable reply in French on behalf of *Prouvost Frères S.A.*

11 You receive letter **K** from Serge Brocard. Write a reply in French of about one hundred words.

 a Thank him for the badge he has sent, but say you cannot return one as they are impossible to obtain.

 b Explain that you are enclosing photographs of badges and of vehicles in use, and that you hope this will satisfy him.

 c Say you feel you cannot accept his gift, and you are therefore returning it with this letter.

I

S.D.M.
10, place de la Victoire,
93100, Montreuil

Montreuil, le 17 juin

World Wide Press,
19, Hastings Walk,
Weymouth,
Dorset.
D74 8TB

Monsieur,

J'ai bien reçu votre lettre du 10 juin et je connais d'ailleurs vos ouvrages.

J'ai bien reçu aussi la lettre de Louis Leconte, mais nous ne faisons pas de publicité car nous faisons simplement un échange avec la revue LA BRETAGNE.

Par contre nous pouvons, si vous le voulez, lorsque votre nouvelle revue sera parue, annoncer sa parution dans la nôtre, gratuitement bien entendu.

Nous serions heureux aussi d'effectuer un échange entre nos deux revues.

Nous vous prions d'agréer, Monsieur, l'expression de nos sentiments distingués,

N. Grenier

J

10 rue Couste,
13104, Montluçon

le 30 mars

Cher Monsieur,

Je viens vous remercier pour le livre 'AU FEU' - je l'ai reçu aujourd'hui.

Je suis collectionneur d'insignes de pompiers et je voudrais vous demander un petit service. Vous trouverez ci-joint l'insigne du Corps des Sapeurs-Pompiers de Paris en échange de votre insigne du Corps de Pompiers que vous portez sur le képi ou sur le casque.

D'avance, je vous remercie et j'aimerais savoir combien je vous dois y compris vos frais d'expédition.

En espérant que ma demande sera prise en considération, je vous prie de croire, avec mes remerciements anticipés, en l'expression de mes salutations les plus cordiales,

Serge Brocard

K

St. Nazaire, le 2 octobre

Monsieur Alain Terieur
10, rue Carnot
44600 St. Nazaire

Prouvost Frères S.A.
2, rue Charles Lamendin
St. Nazaire

Monsieur,

J'ai fait la semaine dernière dans votre magasin l'achat d'un poste de radio. Malheuresement, je ne parviens pas à capter les grandes ondes. Serait- il possible d'effectuer un échange? J'ai bien peur d'avoir égaré la facture, mais j'ai conservé l'emballage.

Le directeur se souvient probablement de moi et je me propose de le rencontrer afin de résoudre ce problème.

Merci de votre compréhension,

Alain Terieur

Newspaper cuttings

In today's paper. . .

This is a summary of the main items found in one issue of *Le Monde*.

1 What news items are discussed on page 48?
2 What are you told about French railway workers?
3 Why is Mr Gorbachev mentioned?
4 Who would you read about on page 12 and why is he in the news?
5 On which pages would you find more foreign news?
6 If you followed soccer where would you look for information?
7 On which pages would you find the weather forecasts and crossword?
8 If you had put an advertisement in this edition of the newspaper, on which pages might it appear?

Le dollar à 7,03 F
PAGE 48

Espagne : élections anticipées
M. Felipe Gonzalez a fixé au 22 juin le scrutin législatif.
PAGE 48

Suppression de 8000 emplois à la SNCF
Un entretien avec M. Philippe Essig.
PAGE 42

Communisme à la prussienne
M. Gorbatchev a rendu hommage au PC est-allemand.
PAGE 6

Les Etats-Unis coupés de l'espace
L'explosion d'une fusée Titan prive les Américains de lanceurs lourds.
PAGE 12

Nouveau patriarche maronite
Mgr Nasrallah Sfeir, élu par le synode de Bkerké, est un homme de compromis.
PAGE 12

Le Monde

ÉCONOMIE

Contre-attaque sur les contrefaçons
La chronique de Paul Fabra
Pages 37 à 40

Débats : Les droits de la personne (2) ● Etranger (3 à 6) ● Politique (7 à 9) ● Société (10 et 12) ● Sports (19) ● Culture (14 et 15) ● Communication (15) ● Economie (42 à 47)

Programme des spectacles (16) ● Radio-télévision (17) ● Informations services : Météorologie, Mots croisés, Loto (17 et 18) ● Carnet (18) ● Annonces classées (20 à 35)

Festival de majorettes

This description of a festival of majorettes appears in the newspaper *La Semaine dans le Boulonnais*:

1 How long will the event last and how many teams will participate?
2 What begins the proceedings and when does this occur?
3 What two different things happen at 3.30 and at 6.00 pm?
4 How much is the entrance fee for spectators?

Festival de majorettes ce week-end dans toute la ville

La société des majorettes saint-martinoises organise samedi 5 et dimanche 6 prochains un festival, auquel participent les majorettes de Fort-Mardylck, Grande-Synthe, Lallaing, La Sentinelle, Leffrincoucke, Le Portel, Lumbres, Marzy, Outreau et Roubaix.

L'ouverture du festival se fera samedi à 17h.30, avec un défilé des majorettes saint-martinoises et des majorettes de Marzy.

Dimanche à 14h.30, les majorettes de Leffrincoucke seront au Mont-Lambert, celles de Lumbres à Ostrohove, celles de Fort Mardyck rue Ch. Gide, celles de Le Portel à la résidence Daunou, celles de Roubaix à la cité Léon Blum, celles d'Outreau au Vallon, celles de la Sentinelle rue G. Boillot, celles de Grande-Synthe rue de Wicardenne et celles de Lallaing, rue Marteau.

A 15h.30, sur le stade municipal, rue au Bois, le concours réunira chaque société. La remise des coupes aura lieu vers 18h. Entrée gratuite.

Les films de la semaine

Look at this newspaper cutting from *Le Monde* and answer the questions.

1. How many of the films listed are French films?
2. Summarise in English the stories behind *Le Serpent, The Strange Affair of Uncle Harry,* and *Alors, Heureux*?
3. Name a police film and also a Western.
4. Which films could a non-French-speaking Englishman follow without difficulty?
5. Which TV channel will be showing the most films?
6. Which night should you stay at home if you want to watch a 'great' film?

Les films de la semaine. Le palmarès de Jacques Siclier.

■ A VOIR
■■ GRAND FILM

DIMANCHE 20 AVRIL

Le Serpent ■

Film français de Henri Verneuil (1972), avec Y. Brynner, H. Fonda, D. Bogarde, P. Noiret, M. Bouquet, M. Held.
TF 1, 20 h 30 (120 mn).

Un transfuge soviétique, membre important du KGB, révèle à la CIA l'existence d'un réseau d'espionnage pour le Kremlin, en Europe occidentale. Vérité ou manœuvre d'intoxication ? Verneuil maintient le suspense d'une partie serrée sur un fil de rasoir. Machination perfectionnée et grands acteurs.

The Strange Affair of Uncle Harry ■

Film américain de Robert Siodmak (1945), avec G. Sanders, G. Fitzgerald, E. Raines, S. Allgood, M. Mac Gill (v.o. sous-titrée. N.).
FR 3, 22 h 40 (80 mn).

En Nouvelle-Angleterre, un célibataire frustré vit avec ses deux sœurs dont l'une, hystérique, veut empêcher son mariage avec une jeune fille dont il s'est épris. Un drame de famille venimeux où rôdent les démons de l'inceste, une étonnante affaire criminelle. Le film s'attira les foudres du Code Hays pour « immoralité » et sa fin fut plusieurs fois remaniée.

LUNDI 21 AVRIL

Alors, heureux ?

Film français de Claude Barrois, Pierre et Marc Jolivet (1979), avec M. Jolivet, P. Jolivet, F. Dougnac, E. Bouix, T. Lhermitte.
TF 1, 15 h 30 (90 mn).

Le fils d'un milliardaire défunt et un paumé, tous deux candidats au suicide, se rencontrent dans un hôpital et poursuivent ensemble leur manie suicidaire. Le comique verbal des frères Jolivet (ils avaient, alors, le vent en poupe à la radio) passe mal l'écran.

Rafles sur la ville ■

Film français de Pierre Chenal (1957), avec C. Vanel, M. Mouloudji, M. Piccoli, F. Guérin, D. Patisson (N.).
TF 1, 20 h 30 (80 mn).

Un inspecteur de police cherche à mettre fin, par tous les moyens, aux activités d'un dangereux truand et séduit la femme d'un collègue débutant. Des personnages sans scrupules d'un côté et d'autre de la barrière. Mise en scène nerveuse, curieuse interprétation.

Sérieux comme le plaisir ■

Film français de Robert Benayoun (1974), avec J. Birkin, R. Leduc, G. Mansart, J.-L. Bideau, P. Etaix, A. Ferréol.
FR 3, 16 h 5 (95 mn).

Deux garçons et une fille formant un harmonieux ménage à trois partent sur les routes à la rencontre du hasard. Fine comédie sur la liberté amoureuse, teintée d'onirisme, de surréalisme.

Le Pistonné ■

Film français de Claude Berri (1970), avec G. Bedos, Y. Robert, R. Varte, N. Demestre, G. Géret, J.-P. Marielle.
FR 3, 20 h 35 (90 mn).

Appelé au service militaire alors qu'il n'a pas envie de s'éloigner de Paris, un jeune homme obtient un « piston » mais se retrouve au Maroc, où le contingent participe à la « pacification ». Dans la série des œuvres autobiographiques de Claude Berri, celle-ci raconte sa vie militaire courtelinesque. Guy Bedos est parfait en bidasse.

MARDI 22 AVRIL

Le Retour du Grand Blond ■

Film français de Yves Robert (1974), avec P. Richard, M. Darc, J. Rochefort, J. Carmet, M. Duchaussoy, P. Le Person.
A 2, 20 h 35 (80 mn).

Le violoniste hurluberlu qui avait été enrôlé malgré lui dans les services secrets français fait les frais de la rivalité de deux officiers. Malgré des astuces de vaudeville et les qualités de l'interprétation, cela ne vaut pas le premier « Grand Blond ». On rit, c'est l'essentiel.

L'Homme de la loi

Film américain de Michael Winner (1970), avec B. Lancaster, R. Ryan, L.-J. Cobbs, S. North, J. Wiseman, R. Duvall.
FR 3, 20 h 35 (95 mn).

Un shérif intransigeant veut absolument – contre l'opinion d'une petite ville, – punir sept hommes responsables d'un meurtre. Douloureuse histoire d'un justicier qui provoque un carnage au nom du devoir, mais dont la mise en scène a subi la mauvaise influence du western italien.

MERCREDI 23 AVRIL

Entends-tu les chiens aboyer ? ■

Film mexicain de François Reichenbach (1974), avec S. Sanchez, A. Camacho, A. de Sade, A. Clavel (v.o. sous-titrée).
FR 3, 22 h 45 (80 mn).

Un Indien venu de la ville cherche un médecin pour son fils malade qu'il porte sur ses épaules. Errance à travers l'espace, le temps, la culture indienne du Mexique, la nature.

JEUDI 24 AVRIL

Le Petit Monde de Don Camillo ■

Film franco-italien de Julien Duvivier (1951), avec Fernandel, G. Cervi, Sylvie (N.).
A 2, 20 h 35 (100 mn).

Dans un village italien de la plaine du Pô, au temps de la « guerre froide », la rivalité d'un curé au tempérament bouillant et du maire communiste. Le premier et le meilleur film d'une série bien connue... qui revient à nouveau.

Frenzy (Frénésie) ■

Film américain d'Alfred Hitchcock (1972), avec J. Finch, B. Foster, B. Leigh Hunt, A. Massey, A. Mc Gowen.
FR 3, 20 h 35 (110 mn).

A Londres, un maniaque sexuel étrangle des femmes. Un innocent est soupçonné, puis arrêté à sa place. Une bonne dose d'humour anglais dans un cocktail de meurtres – dont le spectateur connaît le coupable, – de scènes macabres et d'embrouilles.

VENDREDI 25 AVRIL

Madame porte la culotte ■■

Film américain de George Cukor (1949), avec S. Tracy, K. Hepburn, J. Holliday, T. Ewell, D. Wayne, J. Hagen (v.o. sous-titrée, N.).
A 2, 23 h (100 mn).

Un couple au bonheur sans nuages va se livrer une bataille acharnée au cours d'un procès criminel : lui est substitut du procureur, elle avocate de la défense et féministe. Une comédie brillante et subtile sur le mensonge des rapports sociaux.

Weather map

On a touring holiday in France, your parents buy a newspaper in order to see details of the weather. Since you are the only one in the family who can understand French, your Dad asks you several questions.

1. If you went to the south-east part of the Massif Central on Saturday morning, what sort of weather could you expect?
2. During the afternoon, what will the weather be like in the Bassin parisien?
3. In the afternoon what sort of weather could you expect in the north-west and south-west?
4. What will the temperature be in the Mediterranean area?
5. What is the forecast for Sunday from Brittany down to west Aquitaine?
6. What time of day does the weather map refer to?
7. Look at the map and say what sort of weather you would expect to find in north-west France.
8. What according to the map could your family expect in Paris?
9. Name two countries near France where it would be cloudy.

Evolution probable du temps en France entre le vendredi 25 avril à 0 heure et le samedi 26 avril à minuit.

La situation reste dépressionnaire avec un temps perturbé sur l'Est, instable avec éclaircie à l'ouest.

Samedi matin : sur une moitié est, y compris l'Ile-de-France et le Massif Central, le temps sera très nuageux à couvert avec des pluies. Elles seront encore localement abondantes sur le sud-est du Massif Central et sur les Alpes, en particulier du Sud, modérées sur les autres régions. Sur l'Ouest, les éclaircies domineront.

L'après-midi, une lente amélioration concernera le Bassin parisien, les Ardennes, la Lorraine, le nord de la Bourgogne avec l'éloignement des pluies vers l'est et le développement d'éclaircies. De l'Alsace au Sud-Est, le temps pluvieux persistera. Dans le Nord-Ouest se produiront des averses, quelques-unes également dans le Sud-Ouest. Du Nord-Picardie au Limousin, les éclaricies seront belles.

Les températures seront normales pour la saison, avec des minima de 9 à 12 degrés sur le pourtour méditerranéen, 4 à 8 degrés ailleurs. Les maxima atteindront 12 à 15 degrés en moitié nord, dans le Massif Central et les Alpes, 14 à 19 degrés ailleurs.

Évolution pour le dimanche 27 avril :

La perturbation située sur l'Est donnera encore nuages et pluies, le matin essentiellement sur un quart sud-est, pour se décaler l'après-midi sur le Nord-Est, tandis qu'une amélioration débutera alors sur les régions méditerranéennes.

De la Bretagne à l'ouest de l'Aquitaine, une nouvelle perturbation apportera des pluies faibles seulement.

Entre ces deux zones perturbées, les éclaircies seront prédominantes. Les minima varieront peu. Les maxima baisseront de 1 à 2 degrés.

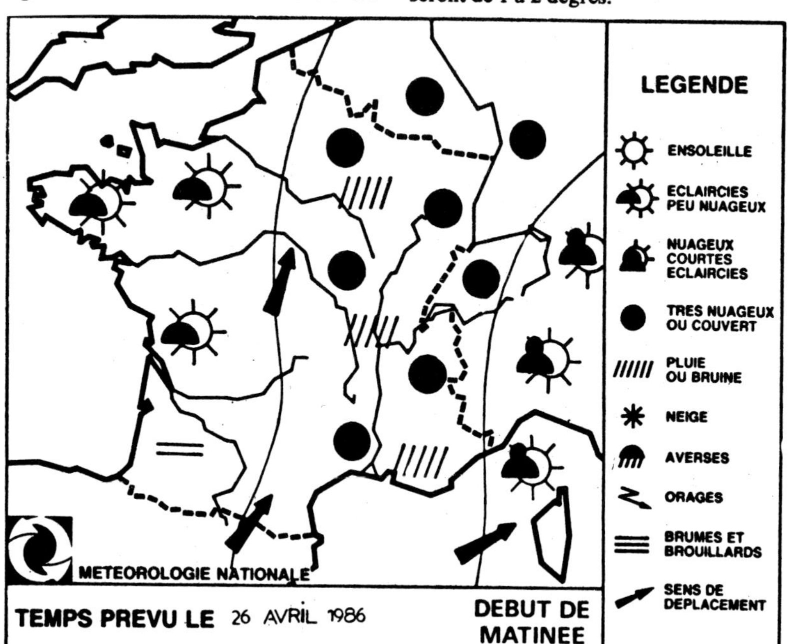

(Document établi avec le support technique spécial de la Météorologie nationale.)

Petites annonces

These advertisements in a French newspaper are placed by people seeking employment or offering work.

Demandes d'emploi

1 Which of these people are interested in work that involves the use of foreign languages?
2 Find an example of someone requiring secretarial employment.
3 How many advertisers would consider *any* form of work?
4 What exactly do the advertisers say about themselves in numbers 1, 4, 7?
5 How many of the advertisers are at school or college?
6 Who requires part-time work?
7 Say exactly what advertisements 2, 5, 6 and 7 mean.
8 You are the lead singer in a French pop group. You notice advertisement 7 and decide to contact the person. Where would you telephone at 9.00 pm?
9 You are an employer looking for personnel. Write to the person in advertisement 4, asking her to arrange a meeting and to send references.

Offres d'emploi

1 Find two vacancies that involve shop work.
2 What exactly are employers saying in advertisements 2 and 6?
3 Give two examples of posts that would be ideally suited to a young girl.
4 Choose either advertisement 6 or advertisement 7 and write a reply to the employer, in French. Remember to set out the letter correctly and to include the appropriate form of ending. Say you saw the advertisement in a newspaper. Give your age and explain why you think you would be suitable for the job.

Demandes d'emploi

1. Etudiante, 20 ans, désirerait travailler dans café à Nice. 3 langues, bonne présentation.
Ecrire au journal No. 1517

2. Jeune fille, 22 ans, suivant cours du soir—dactylographie—cherche emploi de bureau.
Tél. aux heures de repas: 16 1 53 57 13 29

3. Lycéen/étudiant cherche job pour le samedi, un soir par semaine et pendant vacances scolaires. Etudierais toute proposition.
Ecrire au journal No. 1518 qui transmettra.

4. Lycéenne/étudiante—16 ans—cherche travail à mi-temps: garderait enfants le week-end et le soir. Bonnes relations avec enfants. Bonnes références.
15, Bd. Gal de Gaulle, 75006 Paris.

5. Enseignant ne trouvant pas de poste cherche autre emploi. 2 langues, permis poids lourd.
Tél. 33 68 65 10

6. Homme licencié recherche tout emploi—légal. Ecrire au journal No. 2106

7. Chanteur, avec expérience dans groupe pop belge, désire emploi fixe dans groupe français ou dans studio d'enregistrement.
Tél. bureau: 50 36 72 15
Tél. domicile: 60 54 18 80

Offres d'emploi

1. Cherche J.F. pour garder enfants de 16 à 20 heures tous les soirs de la semaine.
Tél. 31 67 06 15

2. Recherche employée de maison dans région parisienne. Références indispensables. Très bon salaire. Nourrie- logée.
Tél. bureau: 16 1 43 05 06 89
Tél. pers. : 16 1 56 05 06 15

3. Recherche fleuriste expérimentée—temps partiel.
Tél. 33 06 29 16

4. Hôtel cherche jeune fille pour ménage et cuisine-nourrie-logée.
Tél. 16 1 32 32 19 18

5. Cherche apprenti charcutier—urgent. Région de Cherbourg.
Tél. 33 15 89 88

6. Embauche coiffeur pour dames. Bonne présentation—expérience vivement souhaitée—CAP coiffure demandé—s'adresser au Salon de coiffure Durand, 15, rue du Canal 44000 Nantes.
Tél. 46 15 82 37

7. Recherche technicien en électroménager, expérience souhaitée. Ecrire au journal No. 1815 qui transmettra.

Les ex-grands bureaux d'Usinor en feu

Loi des séries ? On espère que non. Un incendie a ravagé hier après-midi les combles des anciens grands bureaux d'Usinor où sont maintenant installés cinq nouvelles entreprises. Un sinistre qui arrive onze jours après celui de la carrosserie Behem. Aucun lien entre les deux, mais l'émoi est le même. L'origine du nouvel incendie n'est pas connue, les combles étant dépourvus d'installation électrique et aucun matériel n'y était entreposé.

L'alerte a été donnée vers 14 h 30, par un employé de l'entreprise Loraine Productique services, qui travaillait dans les locaux situés au troisième étage de l'imposant bâtiment, route de Metz. La fumée s'échappait des combles situées dans l'autre aile. La première équipe d'intervention commandée par le lieutenant Würtz du corps des sapeurs-pompiers de Thionville est arrivée au moment où la toiture s'est littéralement embrasée tandis que le panache de fumée s'élevait à plusieurs centaines de mètres. Aussitôt le capitaine Sins, chef de corps, a demandé le renfort des centres de secours de Hayange, Yutz et Terville. La centaine de personnes qui travaillait sur les lieux a été immédiatement évacuée. Des sapeurs-pompiers ont alors attaqué l'incendie aux deux extrémités du bâtiment. Munie d'appareils respiratoires, une troisième équipe pénétrait dans le bâtiment pour accéder directement aux combles.

Le lieutenant Harter, chef du corps de Terville, qui commandait ce dernier groupe a été incommodé par les fumées. Transporté à l'hôpital Bel Air pour examens, il a pu rejoindre ses hommes en début de soirée. Le colonel Dosdat veillait au bon fonctionnement des appareils respiratoires dont ont été largement pourvus les sapeurs-pompiers en raison de l'épaisse fumée qui s'échappait des combles.

Pour alimenter leurs lances, des branchements ont été effectués sur le circuit de la ville et une pompe, avec un débit de 2.000 litres par minute, a puisé l'eau directement dans le ruisseau de Veymerange. De toute façon, pour plus de sécurité, les responsables avaient prévu les tuyaux nécessaires à un second branchement sur la Moselle. Ils n'ont pas eu besoin de les utiliser, la pression étant suffisante.

En moins d'une heure le feu a pu être maîtrisé, le plan d'intervention a montré son efficacité. Les sapeurs-pompiers ont réussi à protéger les bureaux avec des bâches, toutefois les dégâts sont importants. L'eau a envahi de nombreuses pièces. La coupure de courant a eu pour effet la destruction de programmes informatiques, dont se servaient la plupart de ces cinq entreprises de service, installées depuis moins de trois ans, dans ce bâtiment appartenant désormais à la ville de Thionville.

This graphic newspaper account of a fire appeared in the newspaper *Le Républicain Lorrain*.

1. Where did the fire take place and at what time?
2. What had happened eleven days before?
3. Is the cause of yesterday's fire known?
4. Why do you think an electrical fault did not cause the fire?
5. Who raised the alarm and at what time?
6. From where was smoke coming?
7. Who is Monsieur Würtz and what did he see on arrival at the scene?
8. What decision was taken by Captain Sins?
9. How many people were evacuated and how did the first two teams of firemen tackle the blaze?
10. What exactly did the third team of firemen do?
11. What happened to Monsieur Harter and where was he taken?
12. How was water supplied to the firemen?
13. At what rate was the water pumped?
14. What contingency plans for obtaining water were also made?
15. How long did it take to extinguish the fire?
16. In spite of the efforts to reduce water damage what took place?
17. What was the result of cutting off the electrical power?

La gare SNCF étape privilegiée des 'oiseaux migrateurs'

This newspaper article examines problems facing people arriving at Nice railway station.

1. Who are the only people surprised on arrival at Nice station?
2. What has the station hall become?
3. According to the third paragraph why is Nice station like this at night?
4. What job does M. Viollet have?
5. When is the station closed and what are young people then requested to do?
6. Is this problem found only in Nice?
7. How many passengers a day use Nice Station: out of season? in summer?
8. How exactly is the station maintained at night and during the day?
9. Why is there a police station there?
10. What does M. Châtelain say about people who use the station but who do not cause trouble?
11. What routine control do the police exercise and what has been the result?
12. For what two reasons does M. Viollet want to control the seasonal influx of young people?
13. What is the eventual reaction of travellers towards the young people?
14. What practical problems are encountered by young travellers?

Les seuls à s'étonner du spectacle sont les touristes qui débarquent des trains de nuit. Le premier contact nocturne avec Nice a parfois de quoi surprendre. Mais pour les Niçois, le pittoresque de la gare S.N.C.F. "by night" appartient aux bavures inévitables des débordements estivaux. Chaque été voit se renouveler le phénomène. La salle des pas perdus devient une annexe de l'asile de nuit.

Certains guides, paraît-il, conseillent cette halte comme un hébergement possible. De fait, beaucoup de "routards" font de la gare de Nice leur camp de base à leur arrivée sur la Côte.

Quand l'auberge de jeunesse affiche complet, quand les hôtels disponibles se révèlent trop chers, ou tout simplement quand la fatigue les saisit, ces nouveaux voyageurs du rail sortent leur sac de couchage, déplient leur baluchon et s'installent pour la nuit.

● **"Pour la nuit? Pas vraiment,** rappelle le chef de gare adjoint. M. Viollet. **Nous fermons les portes de 1 h à 5 h du matin. Alors, poliment, passé minuit, nous demandons aux jeunes de s'installer plus loin. Ce qu'ils font en déplaçant leur campement... de quelques mètres: sur le parvis et les marches de la gare."**

L'envahissement des bâtiments de la S.N.C.F. par cette encombrante clientèle n'est pas propre à Nice. Toutes les gares du monde, ouvertes aux quatre vents, se plaignent des difficultés d'entretien et de contrôle.

"A Nice, la gare voit défiler près de 60,000 passagers chaque jour. Une clientèle qui double en été. Ce qui double également les problèmes de nettoyage et de sécurité."

Deux équipes d'entretien se relaient pendant la nuit. Dans la journée, une personne est employée à plein temps pour passer la serpillère et vider les cendriers.

La gare est aussi l'un des lieux privilégiés des voleurs à la tire. Ce qui explique la présence d'un poste de police avec deux agents, en permanence, chargés d'assurer la sécurité.

"En ce qui concerne les routards, commente M. Châtelain, directeur départemental des polices urbaines, **nous faisons preuve de compréhension. Tant qu'ils ne créent pas de troubles, nous ne cherchons pas à les chasser. Le plus souvent, nous procédons à des contrôles d'identité. C'est ainsi que dernièrement nous avons appréhendé deux individus recherchés pour des mesures judiciaires."**

Des cas isolés. La plupart des jeunes ne sont pas des "loubards". La direction de la gare n'a d'ailleurs rien de particulier à leur reprocher, hormis cette squaterisation permanente des bancs publics, des consignes et des entrées, ce qui fait un peu désordre dans le décor d'une gare touristique.

"La seule attitude réaliste, conclut M. Viollet, **consiste à tenter de canaliser cette migration saisonnière pour qu'elle ne gêne pas les voyageurs et pas davantage notre service de nettoyage."**

Les touristes choqués par ce laisser-aller estival finissent d'ailleurs par prendre les choses avec le sourire: "On a tous été jeune, convient l'un d'eux, et rêvé d'aventure et de voyages. Le seul problème est que l'aventure se heurte généralement à de sordides détails pratiques tel que le manque d'argent, dénicher un point d'eau, des toilettes, et un coin d'ombre pour poser son sac à dos..."

Jacques BOISSONNET.

Canal +

This article appeared in *Le Monde*:

1 What will happen on April 21st?
2 What will appear on *Canal* + and who is Charles Davies?
3 How is the French view of the British royalty contradictory?
4 Name two of the Queen's good qualities shown in the film.
5 What are you told about events in 1981?
6 What do Europeans find difficult to understand?
7 What positions does the Queen hold in addition to being monarch?

Page 20 – LE MONDE LOISIRS SAMEDI 19 AVRIL 1986

CANAL+

La firme royale

Le 21 avril marquera le soixantième anniversaire de la reine Elisabeth II, souveraine de Grande-Bretagne et d'Irlande du Nord et chef du Commonwealth, ce rassemblement officieux de pays anglophones, ex-colonies britanniques, qui représentent, avec un milliard deux cents millions d'êtres humains, un quart de la population mondiale. Pour fêter cet anniversaire d'une femme remarquable, parce qu'elle incarne une institution millénaire, et sans doute en voie de disparition, la monarchie, Canal Plus va diffuser un documentaire anglais, réalisé par Charles Davies d'après la biographie d'Elisabeth Longford, « Elisabeth II, reine d'Angleterre ».

Il est facile d'ironiser sur cette « Anglaise moyenne », pas très intellectuelle, grand amateur de chevaux, avec un faible pour des chapeaux ridicules. Et les Français ne s'en privent pas, malgré leur nostalgie secrète pour la royauté. Le mérite de ce film – forcément hagiographique – est de montrer les qualités de sérieux, de dévouement, en un mot de classe, chez cette femme qui, depuis l'âge de vingt-cinq ans, représente dignement « la firme royale », comme son père, le roi George VI, avait baptisé avec humour la famille royale.

Le courage n'est pas la moindre de ses qualités, comme l'a montré son attitude face au déséquilibré qui a tiré sur elle en 1981, et, l'âge venant, elle affectionne de plus en plus les bains de foule pour se rapprocher de son peuple. Celui-ci lui rend une admiration et une affection difficiles à concevoir pour les continentaux. C'est que, chef à la fois des armées, de la législature et de l'Eglise, elle symbolise la nation, sans détenir un véritable pouvoir. Un compromis typiquement britannique.

ALAIN WOODROW.

Davantage de touristes et moins de voitures dans ce quartier en métamorphose

LE Vieux-Nice a la cote auprès des touristes. Après la promenade des Anglais, c'est le coin le plus fréquenté par les estivants. Un lèche-vitrines dans les ruelles fraîches, c'est toujours agréable après un bon bain de mer. Cette vogue du Vieux-Nice s'accompagne d'une patiente métamorphose du quartier. Elle est surtout perceptible au niveau des boutiques. Les vieux commerces ont tendance à disparaître pour laisser la place à des magasins dans le vent, parfois super branchés. Peu à peu, le Vieux-Nice devient un endroit « in ». La place Rossetti et le cours Saleya grouillent de jeunes, le soir surtout. Les limonadiers et restaurateurs prospèrent.

A l'origine de ce succès assez récent du Vieux-Nice, il y a surtout la politique de réhabilitation menée depuis plusieurs années. Des entrepôts ont été achetés par la mairie et confiés à des artisans. De nombreux immeubles insalubres ont subi une cure de rajeunissement. Quant aux rues, elles ont été souvent interdites à la circulation des voitures, ce qui permet aux promeneurs de déambuler tranquillement, en toute sécurité. Ce caractère piétonnier du Vieux-Nice devrait s'accentuer au fil des ans. La mairie envisage en effet de supprimer progressivement le trafic routier dans les petites rues. Et même le stationnement. *« Les voitures,* explique M. Raoul Bosio, *n'ont pas leur place ici. Elles constituent parfois des obstacles regrettables, lors des incendies notamment. En deux ans, trois feux très graves ont eu lieu dans des appartements. Les voitures ont considérablement gêné les pompiers. Aucun de ces incendies n'a pu être combattu au pied des immeubles. »*

Mais le stationnement ne peut pas être interdit du jour au lendemain. Il est nécessaire, auparavant, de créer des places de parking qui compensent celles qui seront perdues. Dans cet esprit, un parc autos souterrain est en construction actuellement devant le palais de justice. Un autre est envisagé sur la place Pierre-Gauthier, devant le palais de la préfecture. D'une contenance de trois cents places, il devrait être réalisé en 1988.

Le Vieux-Nice a la cote

This article appeared in *Nice-Matin*:

1 Which two areas of Nice are the most popular with visitors?
2 What is described as enjoyable after swimming in the sea?
3 According to the article what are disappearing and what are replacing them?
4 Who would you be likely to meet in La Place Rossetti and at what time of day?
5 For whom is this good news?
6 What has the town hall purchased and what has been the result?
7 What provision has been made for pedestrians?
8 What problem has parking caused in the last two years?
9 Where is one car park being built and where will another be constructed?
10 How many parking places will this provide in 1988?

La visite du roi Juan Carlos

This extract from *Le Monde* describes Juan Carlos' visit to the UK:

1. According to the caption, what will the visit bring to an end?
2. Whose birthday is mentioned?
3. On which day does the king go to Parliament?
4. What has been the main obstacle to earlier visits?
5. What has not taken place since 1905?
6. Of whom are Juan Carlos and Sophie descendants?
7. Have the Spanish royal couple been to the UK before?
8. What is the significance of 1981 for Anglo-Spanish relations?
9. Why did relations between England and Spain deteriorate after 1969?
10. How did events of 1982 affect both countries?
11. Which international organisation was Spain hoping to join?
12. What agreement was reached in 1984 and how many British citizens were affected?
13. In what way were diplomatic leaders of both countries going to try and promote more co-operation?
14. What happened the month before this report?
15. What role was played by the media?

LA VISITE DU ROI JUAN CARLOS EN GRANDE-BRETAGNE

La fin de la brouille à propos de Gibraltar

De notre correspondant

Londres. – Semaine faste à la cour d'Angleterre. Après la célébration de son soixantième anniversaire, la veille, la reine a accueilli, mardi 22 avril, le roi Juan Carlos d'Espagne, qui, mercredi, devait prononcer un discours au Parlement devant les deux Chambres réunies, privilège accordé pour la première fois dans l'histoire britannique à un monarque étranger.

Cet événement contribue à souligner l'importance particulière d'une visite d'Etat impossible auparavant, car la question de la souveraineté britannique sur Gibraltar y faisait obstacle. Mais, sur ce point, entre Londres et Madrid, une normalisation est maintenant en cours, bien qu'elle se heurte encore à quelques résistances.

Depuis la venue du roi Alphonse XIII, en 1905, aucun chef d'Etat espagnol ne s'était rendu officiellement en Grande-Bretagne. Etroitement lié à la famille régnante britannique – Juan Carlos et la reine Sophie sont, l'un et l'autre, descendants de la reine Victoria, – le couple royal espagnol avait ces dernières années fait de fréquents mais discrets séjours en Grande-Bretagne, à titre strictement privé. Il avait dû renoncer, en 1981, à assister au mariage du prince Charles parce que ce dernier devait commencer son voyage de noces... à Gibraltar.

Surmonter les ultimes difficultés

Les rapports entre l'Espagne et la Grande-Bretagne s'étaient nettement envenimés après 1969, lorsque Franco avait ordonné le « blocus » du Rocher en fermant la frontière séparant celui-ci du territoire espagnol. La guerre des Malouines avait ajouté, en 1982, un nouvel élément de discorde : l'Espagne, entendant préserver ses relations avec l'Amérique latine, n'avait pas soutenu la Grande-Bretagne, et les premières négociations sur Gibraltar avaient été suspendues. Mais la perspective de l'entrée de l'Espagne dans la Communauté européenne, puis la confirmation de l'adhésion à l'OTAN allaient rendre nécessaire un rapprochement.

En novembre 1984, les deux gouvernements ont conclu un accord qui a permis, l'an dernier, la réouverture de la frontière à Gibraltar et le rétablissement partiel des échanges entre ses vingt-cinq mille citoyens britanniques – qui entendent garder cette qualité – et leur voisin espagnol. Londres désirant respecter la volonté des habitants de Gibraltar et Madrid maintenant sa revendication de souveraineté, les discussions se poursuivent avec lenteur.

Cette semaine, les chefs de la diplomatie des deux pays tentent de surmonter les ultimes difficultés sur lesquelles bute la normalisation, par exemple l'utilisation de l'aéroport de Gibraltar par la population espagnole de la région.

Le mois dernier, une « bavure » a failli remettre en cause les progrès en cours : un porte-avions espagnol est venu manœuvrer dans les eaux territoriales contestées à proximité du port. Les deux gouvernements ont préféré ignorer l'incident, tandis que la presse, britannique et espagnole, assurait que l'équipage du navire avait ainsi essayé de « torpiller » la visite à Londres de son souverain...

FRANCIS CORNU.

Changement de cap

This article from *Le Monde* describes the Ivory Coast as a tourist attraction:

1 How long is the flight from Paris?
2 Name two characteristics of the area.
3 What has happened since 1981?
4 How many people visited the Ivory Coast in 1979 and in 1980?
5 What job does M. Gaétan Hervé-Dupenher have?
6 What factors make travel within the country easy for tourists?
7 In 1984 how many rooms and hotels were available for tourists?
8 What two advantages does Grand-Lahou have?
9 Which two water sports are mentioned in the passage?
10 What did the Government decide to do in 1970? Name one way in which it accomplished this.
11 What change has there been in hotel building policy?
12 Name one sort of accommodation being built as an alternative to hotels.
13 Where will development take place in 1987?
14 What change is coming about in the government's involvement in tourism?
15 How will a visit to a Park or Reserve in the Ivory Coast be different from a similar trip elsewhere?

Page 14 – LE MONDE LOISIRS SAMEDI 19 AVRIL 1986

Changement de cap

Vive le tourisme de loisirs.

A six heures de vol de Paris, voici la Côte-d'Ivoire. Sable fin, cocotiers, lagunes, forêt et savane. Une bonne carte de visite sur le marché du tourisme. Jusqu'en 1981, le nombre de visiteurs étrangers n'a cessé de progresser, passant de près de quarante-cinq mille en 1979 à cent quatre-vingt-quatorze mille en 1980. Mais, ici comme ailleurs, la crise a frappé. Moins d'argent, moins de congrès, moins de touristes, les années récentes n'ont pas été les meilleures pour Abidjan. « *Nous relançons la machine et nous avons tout pour réussir* », affirme aujourd'hui M. Gaétan Hervé-Dupenher, responsable de la délégation du tourisme de Côte-d'Ivoire à Paris.

Il est vrai que l'ancienne côte des Bonnes Gens possède de solides atouts pour se faire remarquer. Le pays dispose, en effet, du meilleur réseau routier et ferroviaire de l'Afrique de l'Ouest. Toutes les régions touristiques peuvent également être atteintes par air, avec des possibilités de correspondance sans revenir à Abidjan. A la fin de l'année 1984, la capacité d'accueil de la Côte-d'Ivoire était de dix mille huit cent quatorze chambres réparties dans quatre cent cinquante-deux hôtels. Sur le littoral, Assinie accueille le Club Méditerranée, Grand-Lahou possède le double privilège de la mer et de la lagune pour les amateurs de sports nautiques, Grand-Béréby et Monogaga encadrent les plages de San-Pedro vers la frontière du Libéria. Le pays baoulé, le pays yacouba, le pays senoufo et le royaume agni sont autant d'escapades possibles, loin de la planche à voile ou du ski nautique.

C'est en 1970 que le gouvernement ivoirien a décidé de se donner les moyens nécessaires pour faire de son pays une grande destination touristique. L'Etat est alors hôtelier, restaurateur et agent de voyages. Il crée les infrastructures indispensables pour accueillir ses visiteurs. Il développe notamment le tourisme d'affaires et il est, aujourd'hui encore, parfaitement rodé pour organiser congrès et séminaires. Mais, la crise aidant, les autorités ivoiriennes apprécient de plus en plus l'émergence d'un tourisme de loisirs.

On ne construira plus d'hôtels « cinq étoiles » dont le plus beau fleuron est le fameux Hôtel Ivoire, mais des établissements « une » ou « deux étoiles ». On développera de nouvelles formes d'hôtellerie comme les « auberges villageoises », et les villages de vacances. Enfin, différentes opérations de promotion vont être menées en Europe mais aussi à New-York. Bref, ainsi que le souligne M. Duon Sadia, ministre du tourisme, « *c'est dans le développement d'activités touristiques de loisirs que se trouve l'avenir du tourisme et de l'hôtellerie du pays* ».

Développer les activités de loisirs ? On en parle beaucoup du côté des plages de San-Pedro, à l'ouest d'Abidjan, où un projet d'hôtel-club devrait sortir des cartons au cours de l'année 1987. Cette évolution du tourisme ivoirien se traduit également par un désengagement de l'Etat. Désormais l'investissement privé prend la relève. Mais, à Abidjan, on considère que l'on saura garder son originalité. Ainsi, par exemple, à propos des parcs et des réserves, les responsables du tourisme proposent aux visiteurs une découverte de la faune et de la flore qui s'écarte de l'éternel safari-photo, encadré et morne, en vedette ailleurs.

JEAN PERRIN.

● **Délégation du tourisme de Côte-d'Ivoire, 24, boulevard Suchet, 75016 Paris. Tél. 42-88-62-92.**

Magazine articles

Visiting Great Britain

The shipping company *Brittany Ferries* provides these details in a magazine for French people considering visits to Scotland, Wales and the Lake District.

1 Look at extract **A**.

- **a** What does it tell you about the location of Carlisle?
- **b** What is found along the coast of Scotland?
- **c** What are you told about the valleys and about the mountains?
- **d** Give one detail about: Scottish rivers; the Highlands.
- **e** Is Scottish dancing just for tourists?

2 Read **B**.

- **a** For how long did the Romans occupy Britain? Give two examples of evidence they left behind.
- **b** What, according to the article, is not well known among French people.
- **c** What might you experience when you come across the Roman heritage?
- **d** What are you told about the composition of: the north of England? Northumbria?
- **e** In what way does the last sentence encourage tourism?

3 Study extract **C**.

- **a** Describe the exact location and extent of this region.
- **b** What are the characteristics of the roads, towns and pubs?
- **c** Where would you be greeted with a smile?
- **d** Where would you be likely to find fishermen in this area?
- **e** Name two creatures that might disturb your peace in the Lakes.

A

ECOSSE: GRANDS ESPACES DE LA GRANDE-BRETAGNE.

Au delà de Carlisle (capitale du Lake District) s'ouvre l'Ecosse, pays grandiose, d'abord par la beauté unique de ses panoramas. Interminables chapelets d'îles au large et le long des côtes (plus de 700 îles en tout), bras de mer (firths) tentaculaires tailladant collines et montagnes, vallées (glens) profondes à l'intérieur, lacs (lochs) géants couleur d'acier où se reflètent l'hiver les sommets enneigés et la lande violette l'été, rivières chargées de saumons, sources jaillissantes... L'eau crée ici un spectacle éblouissant, trouant et ciselant avec un talent d'orfèvre. Parmi les plus beaux joyaux, figurent bien sûr les Highlands, ces fameuses "Hautes Terres" qui couvrent la moitié du pays, îles comprises. Mais le spectacle vient aussi du son aigre et troublant, porté par le vent, de la cornemuse; des tourbillons de tartan, quand danse - pas seulement pour le folklore mais pour son plaisir - l'Ecossais en kilt; ***(Suite page suivante).***

B

DE LA FRONTIERE GALLOISE A LA FRONTIERE ECOSSAISE: L'EMPREINTE DES ROMAINS.

Les Romains ont occupé la Grande-Bretagne durant 4 siècles. Aujourd'hui, 2.000 ans plus tard, de nombreux vestiges subsistent, depuis les murailles de Chester jusqu'au Mur d'Hadrien, construit en 122 après Jésus-Christ. C'est cette curieuse et antique Angleterre du Nord, trop mal connue des Français, que nous vous proposons de découvrir.
En partant sur les traces des "colonisateurs" romains, vous éprouverez la sensation merveilleuse de vous retrouver, d'un coup, plus de 20 siècles en arrière.
3 régions composent - outre la Région des Lacs - le Nord de l'Angleterre: le Nord-Ouest (comprenant les Comtés de Cheshire, Lancashire, Great Manchester et Merseyside), le Yorkshire et Humberside, ainsi que le Northumbria (regroupant les Comtés de Cleveland, Durham, Northumberland et Tyne and Wear).
Mais rassurez-vous! L'histoire de ces trois régions ne s'est pas arrêtée à la chute de l'Empire Romain. Et de quelque côté que vous alliez vous ne manquerez pas de choses intéressantes à voir.

C

REGION DES LACS: UN CANADA MINIATURE.

Située au sud de l'Ecosse, isolée de l'Angleterre par la chaîne pennine, la Région des Lacs, petit territoire de 2000 km², est une région sauvage où chaque route a ses secrets, chaque ville ses recoins typiques, chaque pub son ambiance caractéristique. En ces lieux clairsemés de hameaux où l'on vous accueille toujours avec le sourire, vous découvrirez, comme nulle part ailleurs, des forêts rutilantes de couleurs qui flamboyent sous le soleil, dévalent les pentes abruptes que bordent des lacs aux eaux profondes et se mirent dans une onde claire hantée de truites centenaires. C'est ici, paradis des randonneurs, des cavaliers et des pêcheurs que vous découvrirez blottis au fond d'une vallée, cachés derrière une montagne verdoyante ou enveloppés d'un léger brouillard matinal, une multitude de lacs sauvages et attirants, seulement troublés parfois par l'envol des canards et des oies sauvages ou par le cri strident du milan qui prend son essor.

Extracts from a French pop magazine

These pages show some of the letters received by a French pop magazine.

1 How many readers want photographs of their favourite singers or groups?
2 As far as you can tell, how many of the singers/groups are French, or sing in French?
3 Give two examples of letters asking for information about pop stars before they were famous.
4 What exactly is required in letters 5, 6 and 7?
5 Following the example of these letters, write three short notes to the magazine *Disque* enquiring about photographs, albums and concerts by three of your favourite singers/groups.

A

1. Je suis folle de David Essex et je voudrais savoir s'il va venir prochainement à Paris en tournée. J'attends impatiemment ta réponse.

2. Je suis un fan de Madonna et je voudrais savoir combien d'albums elle a sortis jusqu'à présent et si tu peux m'en donner les titres.

3. Je voudrais avoir des renseignements sur Jackie Quartz. Qui est le compositeur du titre "Vivre Ailleurs"? Où est-elle née et depuis combien de temps est-elle connue du public?

4. Salut, je suis un fan d'Indochine. J'aimerais savoir si le chanteur du groupe est vraiment né en Belgique comme le prétendent les journaux? De toute façon, il est génial.

5. Inconditionnel de Michel Jonasz, j'aimerais savoir si vous pourriez me communiquer la liste de ses albums parus en compact-disque et le calendrier de ses concerts en France cette année?

6. Les Fan Clubs de Michel Berger et de France Gall organisent le 20 juin une soirée-concert à Toulouse dans la salle des fêtes. Pouvez-vous me dire si Michel et France seront là et, si oui, comment me procurer un billet?

7. A la suite de votre article sur Bernard Lavillier je tiens à apporter la précision suivante: il commentera lui-même le prochain reportage sur le Carnaval de Rio sur Antenne 2. La nuit sera chaude. Amateurs, à vos cassettes!

8. J'adore Francis Cabrel et j'aimerais avoir une photo dédicacée de lui. Pouvez-vous me donner l'adresse de son Fan Club? Merci.

9. Ma meilleure amie adore le groupe Queen, aussi pour son anniversaire j'aimerais lui offrir une photo dédicacée. Pourriez-vous m'indiquer l'adresse de leur fan club en France?

Le pays du sport roi

The English love of sport is described in this magazine article. You are discussing it with a French penfriend who is staying at your home:

1. Which two sportsmen are mentioned?
2. What do you understand by 'le jeu d'équipe'?
3. According to the writer, where will pupils spend a lot of time once they are adults?
4. Name three activities that go on at country clubs.
5. What is the French expression for 'social life'?
6. Name one thing you may find in a park.
7. What do amateur sportsmen really like?
8. Who may you see in the streets?
9. What would they hold up over their heads?
10. Name two sports stadia and the sports you would find there.

LE PAYS DU SPORT ROI.

Plus que tout autre peuple, les Britanniques ont intégré le sport à leur façon de vivre. Ecoliers ou étudiants, la balle de cricket, la raquette de tennis ou la crosse de hockey sur gazon seront toujours associés à leur livres et à leurs cahiers.

CLUB HOUSE ET COMMONS.

Ce n'est pas vraiment le désir de produire des athlètes en série, de la stature des Sebastien Coe ou des Kevin Keagan, qui pousse nos amis anglais à taper dans un ballon ou à échanger des balles sur les terrains de sport de l'école. . . Non ! c'est bien plutôt l'apprentissage de la vie en commun. Le jeu d'équipe crée l'esprit d'équipe! D'où le fameux "fair play" britannique, bien réel, qui régne dans tous les domaines sportifs et trouve sa place même au milieu des pires empoignades. Jusque dans le sport, on retrouve, de ce côté-ci de la Manche, une certaine idée de ce que doit être la Civilisation.

Devenus adultes, nos jeunes écoliers concentreront beaucoup d'activités au sein du "club house" du country-club. Cette institution, à la patine un peu désuète, provinciale, reste cependant un lieu de rendez-vous privilégié. On vient y boire un verre, célébrer une fête, se souvenir d'un anniversaire. On y joue au bridge, bien sûr.

Toujours entouré de courts de tennis, de parcours de golf, de plans d'eau et de biens d'autres installations sportives. Plutôt cossus, ces "club-houses" jouent un rôle non négligeable dans la "social life" (la vie communautaire) des Anglais. Les "commons", plus populaires, exercent la même fonction: des enfilades de pelouses parsemées, çà et là, de cages pour "goal keeper" de football ou de poteaux de rugby, permettent aux enfants du quartier, et aux plus âgés, de se retrouver.

LES GRANDS TEMPLES DU SPORT.

Sportifs amateurs, amoureux du grand air et du "challenge", les Britanniques sont aussi des passionnés de sport professionnel. Les longues et bruyantes processions des supporters d'une équipe de football, (celle du "Kop" de Liverpool, par exemple) dans les rues de la ville, étonnent toujours. Surtout cette habitude de brandir à bout de bras une écharpe tricotée aux couleurs du club ainsi soutenu!

Chaque grand rendez-vous sportif est une fête, une cérémonie, qu'il faut au moins avoir vue une fois dans sa vie. . . et chaque sport a son temple! Pour le football, c'est Wembley à Londres et pour le rugby c'est Twickenham, dans le sud-ouest de la capitale, près de Richmond: sans oublier le célèbre Arms Park de Cardiff, au Pays de Galles, ou Murrayfield, en Ecosse.

Pour le tennis, c'est Wimbledon. Le cricket, lui, se partage à Londres deux lieux saints: Oval, au sud de la Tamise, en face de Westminster, ou Lords, le long de Regent's Park. Sport typiquement anglo-saxon, le cricket donne lieu chaque année à une formidable rencontre au sommet entre l'Angleterre et l'Australie. Les sports automobiles et motocyclistes, eux, se déroulent hors de la capitale: à Silverstone ou Brands Hatch, et à l'île de Man pour le très connu "Tourist Trophy" motocycliste.

Les amateurs de bateau ne manqueront pas d'assister aux Régates d'Henley et à la "Cowes Week" de l'île de Wight, début août. Les passionnés d'aviation iront lever le nez au "Farnborough Air Show" début septembre, dans cette petite ville du Hampshire. Et naturellement, les inconditionnels de la race chevaline, turfistes ou non, braqueront leurs jumelles à Ascott ou Epsom.

Londres, l'occident et l'orient réunis

This account of London is intended to encourage French people to visit the capital.

1 Which cities are bigger than London?
2 How many people live in London?
3 What coexists happily with traditional British customs?
4 What headgear is likely to be seen on passers-by?
5 What drinks are popular in pubs and what is said about opening hours?
6 Which two famous buildings are mentioned?
7 What would visitors do in Knightsbridge?
8 State two nationalities that are represented in the restaurants.
9 Name four modes of transport available.
11 Are modern and classical musical tastes catered for?
11 What is the advantage of London Transport travel cards?
12 How would further information on London Transport be obtained?

LONDRES. L'OCCIDENT ET L'ORIENT REUNIS.

Pour vous dépayser, inutile d'aller très loin. Allez à Londres. Cette gigantesque métropole - la première d'Europe et la troisième après New York et Tokyo - qui héberge plus de huit millions d'habitants de toutes couleurs, races et religions, excerce sur ses visiteurs (comme d'ailleurs sur ses habitants) une fascination unique, proche de l'envoûtement. Toutes les différences qui peuvent exister sur la terre, et toutes les folies semblent s'être donné ici rendez-vous. Néanmoins, l'exotisme et les excentricités de Londres font bon ménage avec les coutumes et les traditions britanniques. D'où l'atmosphère étrange et inhabituelle qui règne dans cette ville carrefour. Foule disparate et colorée déferlant sur les trottoirs des rues marchandes où le shopping est roi, défilés de Rolls, chapeaux melons vissés sur les têtes rubicondes typiquement anglo-saxonnes, sombres taxis d'allure "rétro", bus rouge sang à impériale, foot-guards impassibles sous leur drôle de bonnets à poils, thés feutrés l'après-midi dans les salons, mais flots de bière et de whisky dans les pubs, (attention, ils n'ouvrent qu'à certaines heures), bonnes manières et manières fantaisistes, ingénuité et rouerie des anglais, flegme apparent et passion rentrée, parcs délicieusement calmes et fureur dans les rues, voilà Londres. Une ville de paradoxes, merveilleusement absurde, terriblement conventionnelle et malgré tout débridée.

Londres: une ville magique où tout est possible.

Visitez bien sûr les grandes curiosités officielles, depuis la cathédrale St-Paul jusqu'à la Tour de Londres. Faites du shopping à outrance, notamment dans les célèbres rues de West End comme Oxford Street, Regent Street, Picadilly, Bond Street, Knightsbridge, Kings Road... Courez les restaurants anglais, chinois, indiens, japonais, français, africains... Nichez dans les petits hôtels confortables et économiques ou chez l'habitant dans un "bed and breakfast" (pour encore moins cher). Sillonnez Londres en bateau (sur la Tamise), en métro, en bus, en train, en taxi (louez-en un pour la journée) plutôt qu'avec votre voiture. Plongez dans l'univers des pubs, des concerts "pop" ou classiques des grandes manifestations artistiques, culturelles, sportives (il y en a en permanence), sans oublier le dédale inextricable des ruelles de Soho, village de plaisirs interlopes. Il y a tout ce que l'on veut à Londres.

Les transports londoniens.

Vous pouvez vous procurer une carte de libre circulation (métro+autobus à impériale) valable 1, 3, 4 ou 7 jours afin de vous déplacer dans Londres. Pensez-y car ce genre de forfait peut vous faire faire bien des économies! Renseignements pour les London transports au 01.222.1234... on vous y informera en Français si vous le souhaitez!

Letters to a teenage magazine

These letters appeared in a French magazine popular with teenage girls.

Letter 1

- **a** What was the writer's first impression of her colleague?
- **b** What did she later learn that her colleague had done?
- **c** What does the writer not wish to do?
- **d** Put the last three sentences into English.

Letter 2

- **a** What information is given in the first sentence?
- **b** What two qualities is the second person alleged to possess?
- **c** Why might the writer of the letter be embarrassed at school?
- **d** How has the writer tried to solve her problem?

Letter 3

- **a** Give one reason why the writer must work hard at school.
- **b** In English, explain 'le problème'.
- **c** How much time a week does the writer devote to this other activity?
- **d** Who is going to write to her parents, and why?
- **e** How have things been at school until now?
- **f** What question is raised in the final sentence?

Letter 4

- **a** Summarise the first paragraph in your own words.
- **b** What is the writer's attitude towards her mother?

Letter 5

- **a** Which part of France does the writer hope to visit and with whom?
- **b** What does her mother say and what would she prefer the girl to do?
- **c** What does the writer feel about family holidays?
- **d** Translate the last sentence.

Letter 6

- **a** What do the writer's friends do?
- **b** Why do they laugh at her and what do they say about her relationship with boys.
- **c** Write a 50-word reply in French, giving the writer some practical advice.

Letter 7

- **a** Name one thing that happens to the writer of this letter at school.
- **b** What must she do each week—how does she manage to do this?
- **c** How does the situation affect the girl at night?

Letter 8

In French, write a reply of about 60 words to this letter.

1 J'ai 17 ans, et je travaille le samedi dans un supermarché où je suis devenue amie avec une fille qui me semblait bien au premier abord. Je l'ai déjà invitée chez moi, mais j'ai appris depuis qu'elle volait de l'argent dans la caisse au supermarché. Je ne voudrais pas la faire renvoyer mais je pense que c'est très mal de sa part de prendre ainsi de l'argent. A qui dois-je en parler? Dois-je ne rien dire à personne? Que pensez-vous de mon idée de lui dire que les patrons soupçonnent des voleurs parmi le personnel?

2 Mon copain vient de me quitter pour ma meilleure amie. Il prétend qu'elle est plus amusante que moi et aussi plus jolie. C'est très contrariant car elle est dans la méme école que moi, et tous les copains semblent être au courant de la situation. Que dois-je faire? J'ai pensé me mettre au régime et j'ai essayé de me faire d'autres amis pour oublier mon copain. Est-ce la solution? Aidez-moi!

3 Cette année c'est le Bac, et je vais devoir beaucoup travailler si je ne veux pas redoubler ma terminale et louper mon Bac. Le problème, c'est que des copains m'ont demandé de jouer de la guitare dans leur groupe, qui se produit dans les maisons de jeunes et les églises, de la région Nantaise. Ce qui veut dire que je devrai répéter une fois par semaine et jouer en concert deux fois par semaine. Le proviseur de mon lycée va écrire à mes parents à ce propos car il pense que cela m'empêchera de travailler convenablement. Jusqu'à présent tout se passe bien et j'ai toujours eu les meilleures notes les années précédentes. J'ai donc bon espoir pour le Bac. Je me demande si le proviseur a le droit de m'empêcher de jouer dans ce groupe?

4 J'ai découvert que mon beau-père fréquente une autre femme deux fois par semaine. Je les ai vus dans un café près de chez moi et j'ai remarqué qu'ils se tenaient la main. Il semblerait que cela dure depuis six mois, mais je n'en ai parlé à personne jusqu'ici.

J'espère que ce sera bientôt fini et je suis vraiment désolée pour ma mere. Je ne sais vraiment pas quoi faire. Pouvez-vous m'aider?

5 J'ai 16 ans et j'aimerais partir en vacances dans le Midi avec 3 amies. Ma mère prétend que je suis trop jeune pour ce genre de vacances et veut que j'aille avec la famille au Touquet. Je trouve les vacances en famille très ennuyeuses car mes parents ne me laissent pas aller en boîte faute d'amies pour m'accompagner. Ne pensez-vous pas qu'une fille de mon âge devrait pouvoir passer dix jours de vacances avec trois copines d'école?

6 J'ai 14 ans, je suis en 3ème au collège de Lavien. Mes amies sortent avec des garçons alors que moi je suis toujours toute seule. Elles se moquent un peu de moi car j'ai quelques boutons sur la figure et elles disent que c'est à cause de cela que les garçons ne me regardent pas. Personne ne m'aide et mes copines me laissent toute seule. Que dois-je faire?

7 J'ai 15 ans, à l'école, quatre filles de terminale m'embêtent tout le temps, elles me tapent, vident mon cartable et abîment mes affaires. Elles m'ont demandé de l'argent et elles m'ont dit qu'elles ne m'embêteront plus. Alors chaque semaine, je leur apporte 30 francs mais le problème est que je suis obligée de les voler à mes parents ou à mes grands-parents.

Je n'ose pas leur dire, encore moins à mes professeurs. Plus cela va, plus j'ai peur; et je n'arrive plus à dormir la nuit. Je suis vraiment désespérée. Que me conseillez-vous de faire? A qui dois-je en parler?

Je suis absolument incapable d'aller voir la police.

8 Ma meilleure amie m'a invitée à dormir chez elle, elle habite à environ 20 km. de chez moi. Ses parents seront partis en week-end donc nous serons toutes les deux seulement. Mais mes parents ne veulent pas que j'aille chez elle car ils pensent que c'est un prétexte pour sortir tard, pour rencontrer des garçons et aller dans les cafés.

Ce n'est pas juste, j'ai 17 ans et je ne suis plus une petite fille! Que pensez-vous de l'attitude de mes parents? Trouvez-vous que c'est normal qu'ils ne veuillent pas que j'aille chez elle?

Recettes

On holiday in France you purchased a copy of *Marie-France,* containing these recipes. You decide to try out some recipes and discuss them with your Mum. Since she cannot speak French you have to be particularly helpful. Why not try a couple yourself?

1. For each recipe make a list of the ingredients in English.
2. You decide to translate the recipes for your Mum—summarise the four sets of instructions in English so she can follow them easily. You will not have to put every word into English.
3. You decide to send a copy of your favourite English recipe to a French pen friend. Using the format shown in 'Marie-France' give a list of ingredients and simple instructions in French.

JARRET DE VEAU SOUBISE

Pour 6 personnes : ■ 6 tranches de jarret de veau. ■ farine. ■ 750 g d'oignons. ■ 50 g de beurre. ■ 2 cuil. à soupe d'huile. ■ 1 cuil. à café de sucre. ■ 50 g de beurre. ■ 25 g de crème. ■ 1 verre de vin blanc. ■ Sel, poivre.

Farinez les tranches de jarret et faites-les dorer à la cocotte dans l'huile et le beurre chaud. Ajoutez-le vin blanc et 1 verre d'eau. Couvrez, laissez cuire 1 h 30 à 2 h. Pendant ce temps épluchez les oignons. Faites-les cuire 10 minutes à l'eau bouillante. Egouttez. Passez-les à la moulinette ou au moulin-légumes.
Dans une poêle faites fondre 50 g de beurre. Ajoutez une cuillerée à café pleine de farine, tournez jusqu'à obtenir un mélange moussant et coloré. Ajoutez les oignons, mélangez, laissez cuire jusqu'à obtenir une purée onctueuse. Ajoutez le sucre en poudre cuit en caramel ce qui renforcera le goût et la couleur de la purée. Salez, poivrez, ajoutez la crème fraîche. On peut accompagner de croûtons frits.

ESCALOPES AU POIVRE VERT

Pour 6 personnes : ■ 6 escalopes un peu épaisses. ■ 50 g de beurre. ■ 1 cuil. à soupe d'huile. ■ 1 pot de crème fraîche. ■ 1 boite de poivre vert au naturel. ■ Vin blanc. ■ 500 g de champignons de Paris. ■ 50 g de beurre.

Dans une sauteuse faites dorer rapidement les escalopes des deux côtés. Ajoutez 1/2 verre de vin blanc. Couvrez la sauteuse au 3/4, laissez cuire 15 mn. Pendant ce temps faites rapidement sauter les champignons à la poêle dans le beurre chaud. Egouttez le poivre vert, rincez-le à l'eau fraîche, écrasez au pilon dans un mortier, mélangez-le à la crème fraîche.
Tenez les escalopes au chaud dans la sauteuse, versez crème et poivre vert, les champignons, laissez réchauffer. Versez sur les escalopes. Servez avec des pâtes.

CÔTES DE VEAU À LA SICILIENNE

Pour 6 personnes : ■ 6 côtelettes de veau épaisses dans le filet. ■ 12 petits oignons. ■ 250 g de lard de poitrine fumée. ■ Un poivron vert. ■ Un poivron rouge. ■ 1 verre de vin blanc. ■ 1/2 pot d'olives vertes ou noires dénoyautées.

Dans une sauteuse faites dorer les oignons et le lard coupé en lardons, les poivrons en lamelles. Couvrez de la moitié du vin blanc et laissez cuire couvert jusqu'à évaporation. Videz la sauteuse, farinez légèrement les côtelettes, faites-les dorer sur les deux faces. Remettez dans la sauteuse avec légumes, lardons et le reste du vin blanc. Salez légèrement. Couvrez, laissez cuire 20 minutes à feu doux. 5 minutes avant la fin de la cuisson, ajoutez les olives vertes égouttées et pochées 5 minutes à l'eau bouillante. Servez avec du riz ou des pâtes.

RÔTI AUX OLIVES

Pour 6 personnes : ■ 1 rôti dans la noix ou le quasi de 1,250 kg environ. ■ 1 os de veau. ■ 50 g de beurre. ■ 2 oignons. ■ Sel, poivre. ■ 1 pot d'olives vertes dénoyautées.

Dans le beurre chaud avec une cuillerée d'huile faites dorer le rôti à la cocotte sur toutes ses faces. Ajoutez l'os de veau, l'oignon finement émincé. Salez. Ajoutez un verre d'eau. Couvrez, laissez cuire 1 bonne heure à petit feu en retournant la viande de temps en temps. Egouttez les olives. Rincez-les à l'eau fraîche. Pochez-les 5 mn à l'eau bouillante. Egouttez-les. Ajoutez-les dans la cocotte 15 mn avant la fin de la cuisson. Poivrez. Servez avec des bulbes de fenouil cuits à l'eau, égouttés et étuvés au beurre.

Musée de l'automobiliste

1 Name two ways in which vehicles are grouped at the museum.
2 Why are the cars not simply relics?
3 Some cars have famous names. Give two examples of these names. How have other cars made their mark?
4 What happens each year?
5 The third paragraph mentions some events. Give three examples.
6 Where is the museum located and what accommodation is provided for visitors?
7 What should motorists heading for Nice look out for?
8 Is the museum closed for lunch? When is it open during October?
9 Work out the entry fee for two adults and two children.

Le musée de l'Automobiliste procède d'un parti pris architectural qui a su allier la beauté du site et le fonctionnalisme des salles d'exposition. Les automobiles sont regroupées, soit par marque, soit par genre, ou mises en situation dans un environnement constitué d'accessoires d'époque.

Les voitures exposées à Mougins sont toutes capables de prendre la route. La plupart portent des noms prestigieux comme Bugatti ou Ferrari, quelques-unes ont participé à des courses célèbres. Toutes ont marqué une époque. Chaque année, deux expositions thématiques soulignent un aspect caractéristique de l'automobile.

De nombreuses animations sont organisées : concentration de voitures anciennes, concours d'élégance, ventes aux enchères publiques, bourses d'échanges, manifestations qui font de ce Musée un centre d'activité exceptionnel.

Le musée de l'automobiliste est situé en bordure de l'autoroute A 8 — entre Antibes et Cannes — Aire des Bréguières. De larges parkings sont aménagés, directement accessibles de l'autoroute. Provisoirement, pour les automobilistes se dirigeant vers Nice, un itinéraire fléché peut être suivi en empruntant la sortie Cannes, direction Mougins.

PARKING — CAFÉTÉRIA — LIBRAIRIE AUTOMOBILE
BOUTIQUE CADEAUX — MODÉLISME — JOUETS
MAQUETTES — CINÉMA

OUVERT TOUS LES JOURS SANS INTERRUPTION

1er avril/30 sept. : 10 heures/19 heures
1er oct./31 mars : 10 heures/18 heures

PRIX D'ENTRÉE 25 F **Enfants et groupes 15 F**

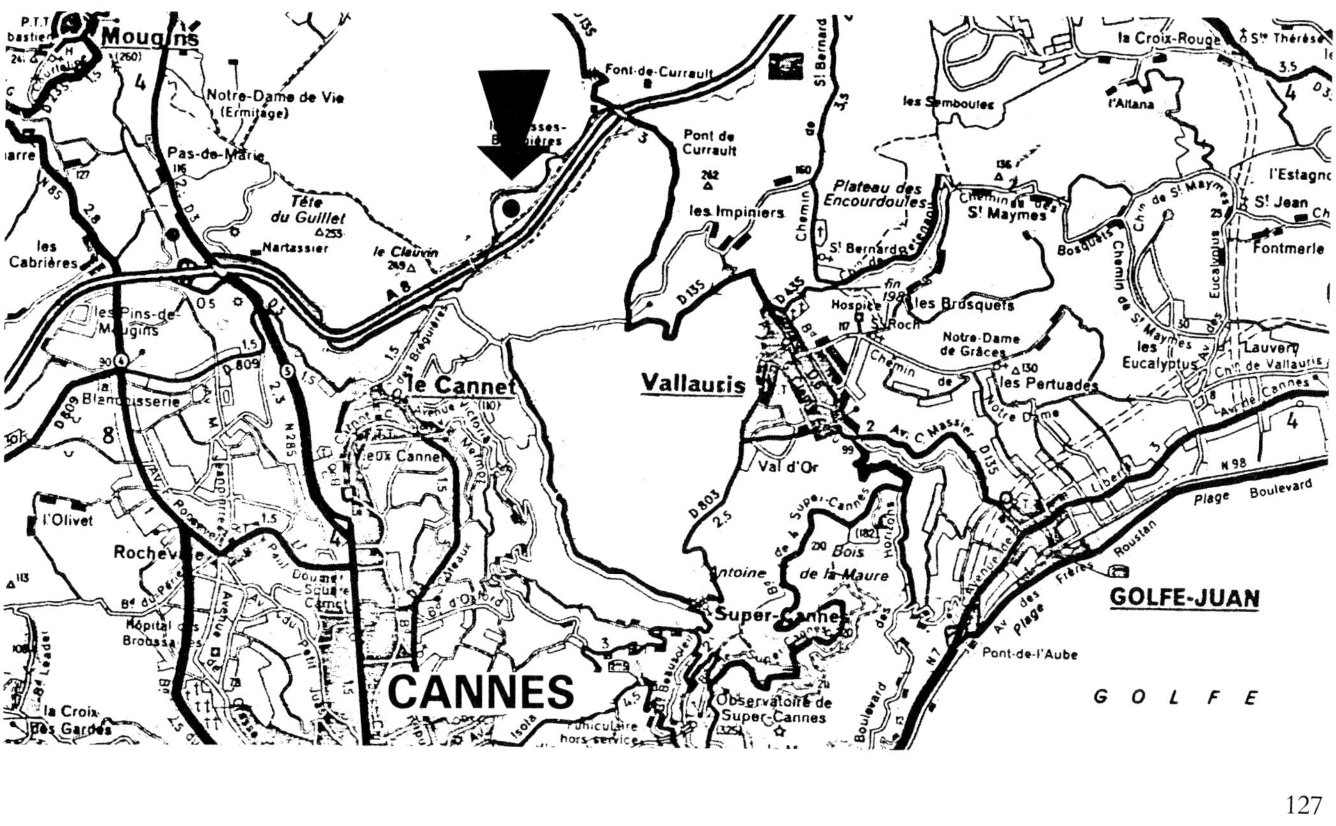

Application of the material

Page	Public notices & signs	Advertisements & announcements	Timetables & tickets	Guides & brochures	Menus & lists	Letters	Newspaper articles	Magazine articles
Motoring	√							
Bus Travel	√	√	√	√				
Railway Travel	√		√	√				
The Metro and RER	√		√	√				
Air Travel	√	√	√	√				
Travel by Sea	√	√		√				
Tourist Office and Customs	√	√		√				
Banking	√	√						
Food and Drink	√	√		√	√		√	
Shops and Markets	√	√			√			
Entertainment	√	√			√		√	√
School	√	√				√	√	
Holidays	√	√		√	√		√	
Emergencies	√	√	√	√			√	
Postcards			√			√		
Informal Letters						√		
Formal Letters						√		
Newspaper Cuttings		√				√	√	
Magazine Articles					√	√		
Further Extracts		√			√			√
				√				